FREEDOM AND ORDER

By the same author:

Industrial Democracy
The Atlantic Management Study
Government and Enterprise in Ireland
In Good Company
Out on Their Own
Boardroom Practice
Talking to Ourselves

FREEDOM AND ORDER

Studies in Strategic Leadership

Ivor Kenny

Oak Tree Press
Dublin

Oak Tree Press
Merrion Building
Lower Merrion Street
Dublin 2, Ireland
www.oaktreepress.com

A catalogue record of this book is
available from the British Library

ISBN 1 86076 120 8

Printed in Britain by MPG Books
Bodmin, Cornwall

For the Family

Maureen

Dermot and Geraldine
Maeve, Grace and Dermot

Conor and Judith

Ivor and Karen
Alex

Helen

Mark

TABLE OF CONTENTS

ACKNOWLEDGEMENTS

There are many people without whose participation this book would not have seen the light of day.

First the chief executives and their colleagues, all 480 of them, who took part in the Studies recounted here.

Professor Gordon Wills, President of the International Management Centres, came from Buckingham to stay in a B&B in Dublin and sit on my neck until I had begun the D.Litt. thesis on which the book is based.

Tony Farmar put order on a mass of writing accumulated over the years.

David Givens of Oak Tree Press showed me shortcomings instantly recognisable once he had pointed them out. Brian Langan was a meticulous editor. Remaining faults are my own.

Dr Richard Teare in Oxford was my internal examiner for the D.Litt. and Professor Tony Cunningham in Dublin my extern. My thanks for their searching criticisms and for their kindly support.

I am indebted to University College Dublin for providing me with a lair from which to venture into the world of praxis and to which to return to gather my thoughts.

Lastly my thanks to my friend and colleague of 11 years in UCD, Gillian Acton, who shoulders any burden with a smile.

There are truths on this side of the
Pyrenees that are falsehoods on the other.

— Blaise Pascal

And if the world were black or white entirely
And all the charts were plain
Instead of a mad weir of tigerish waters,
A prism of delight and pain,
We might be surer where we wished to go
Or again we might be merely
Bored but in brute reality there is no
Road that is right entirely.

— Louis MacNeice

PREFACE

*Successful theory is merely that which enables him who is
suitably armed to carry through successful practice.*

— Reg Revans

The bones of this book are a series of Studies carried
out with major Irish enterprises over the past 15 years
or so. I have tried without much success to avoid the
title "consultant" because it has connotations I don't
particularly like. I have used the softer term "adviser".
Having written the book, adviser looks threadbare: I try
not to give advice and frequently fail. University pre-
fixes such as Professor (or Senior Research Fellow, my
sonorous style and title in UCD) act as barriers in the
business world. Two young entrepreneurs invited me
to be chairman of their company. At the end of the in-
troductory lunch, one turned to the other and said with
relief, "You know, he's normal".

I use the term "Study", rather than, say, consultancy
assignment or intervention, because (a) I work from a
university and the word Study is more appropriate
(and genteel) and (b) because they *are* research studies.

From the organisation's point of view, they are about helping it get a clearer picture of where it is and where it's going. From my point of view, they stem from an enduring curiosity about organisations and how they work, from an abiding belief that the more organisations make people unfree, the worse they function.

The book had its origins in a thesis for the degree of Doctor of Letters. Whatever its merits or shortcomings for the discipline of the doctorate, it was a personal experience. It caused me to go back over much of my working life, to identify the different threads, to see if they could be pulled together to give a pattern, to see if there was progress — learning — or had I been like the courtiers of Louis XIII, forgetting nothing and learning nothing?

It also caused me to read around the subject, something I had done with little discipline over the years. Casual reading is easily forgotten. Purposeful reading is a joy. It was particularly cheerful in the context of the thesis because it confirmed that I was on the same ladder as seriously distinguished authors, if some rungs behind them.

Action learning must surely be about finding out that you are not as good as you think you are — or not so bad either.

The purpose and method of the work are described in detail in Chapter 2. Chapter 3 is about the chief executives of the organisations studied. CEOs are the primary "client". Without their trust and commitment, Studies would never get off the ground. This is followed by seven Studies, Chapters 4 to 10. Chapter 11 gives very short summaries of five other Studies, the nature of whose business was so specific as to make them identifiable if they were described in any detail. Nevertheless, they show a remarkable similarity in their analyses.

Perhaps that is the key to the book. If you work intimately with a number of different organisations, in different countries, with different products, in different markets, with different ownership structures — state and private — with different histories and styles, and if their diagnoses of their problems are the same, then there is something worth passing on. I believe that what has been learned from the Studies is of general application, at least in Western democracies. (The only depressing experiences I've had were in the Soviet Union under the corrupt regime of Brezhnev, where people were truly unfree, and in 1994 in the Czech Republic, where the rotten Communist legacy had left fear and suspicion in managers' minds: it will take a generation before they are liberated.)

A Study takes about nine months to complete, depending on the number of managers involved. A minimum of 20 participants is needed: after the twentieth interview, the issues are clear. Why continue then with up to 30 more interviews? More important than getting the issues clear — and they are seldom surprising — is that the Study gives to every senior manager an opportunity to take an active part in the process. And, through the written *Reports*, it gives the chief executive the opportunity to hear the undiluted views of the entire management team. The power of the consensus that emerges is the unique power of the Study. No one could walk away from it with their fingers in their ears. A Study is designed to bring considerable pressure on the whole team to take action. Studies are a form of *action* research, *action* learning — not a theoretical exercise.

A cynic might say there are only two questions you need ask when you enter an organisation: *How long have you been here?* and *What harm has it done you?* Organisations can do awful things to people. As the story unfolds, you will see that I steer clear of awful organisations. I have nothing to offer them, and they certainly have nothing to offer me.

I hate management by slogan, but let me risk one because it's close to the heart of the matter. *Efficiency comes (only) from enthusiasm.* Of course, we should be intolerant of inefficiency but you can't enforce enduring efficiency. If you try to, people will find ways to walk up and down your back. Imposed efficiency cannot last. Inherent efficiency, where people *see* the problems and solve them themselves, is lasting efficiency. That can come only from enthusiasm. Enthusiasm can come only from participation or, to use a vogue word, ownership. The essence of Kafka's labyrinthine bureaucracies is that nobody accepts responsibility for anything. If people are not given responsibility, how can they be expected to behave responsibly? Studies, as we shall see, are about encouraging shared responsibility. The prerequisite for shared responsibility is a shared knowledge of what's really going on.

What I like most about managers is their ordinariness — in the most positive sense of the word. Their principal concern is *doing*, getting on with the job. Most of them are worldly-wise and tolerant. The best of them have an impressive instinctive wisdom. A few indulge in bad or conspicuous behaviour but usually get found out: management depends on results, not nastiness or flimflam.

Nietzsche said the crowd was untruth. That is the élitist view. An élitist could dismiss a Study by describing it as a sharing of ignorance. Two things about that. First: *nobody* knows more about an organisation than the people who work in it. Second: of course an organisation may need the cool judgement of a consultant on technical problems. I have encouraged the commissioning of a consultant on, say, strategic process. Or, a familiar problem: how to conduct staff assessments, something to which many if not most organisations have an aversion — assessments are carried out mechanically or not at all. Or, how to improve information technology, a perennial problem, or the quality of production methods . . . the list is endless. But nobody knows the *management* issues of an organisation better than the people who see them every day. A list of issues from various Studies is given near the beginning of Chapter 2 (pp. 56–7).

It would be disingenuous to pretend the work is intellectual flypaper, gathering views and summarising

them. I conduct a maximum of eight interviews a week,
Monday to Thursday, two a day. It took me a while to
understand why they were so tiring. It was not the time
involved — that passes quickly. It was the absolute
concentration on what the interviewee was saying (or
meaning). An interviewee will detect instantly if you
are not listening and then the vital bond of trust is broken, almost irrecoverably. The essence of the interview
is that the interviewee feels that you understand and
sympathise with what he or she is saying. Some inter-
viewees start talking before they sit down. Others need
a warm-up before the ideas flow. Occasionally, an interviewee gets stuck and needs a helping hand. I have
never met anybody who told deliberate lies. They may
exaggerate or paint doom-laden pictures, but a smile
and "Do you really mean that?" restore an even keel.

Studies are always the same and always different.
The motivation comes from the difference. While key
issues, such as unclear strategy, no strategic process or
minimal communication are now familiar, the organisations are different and, like fingerprints, the people
who constitute them are different. The day a new Study
begins is a sunny day. Conversely, there is a time to
part. The corruption of consultancy is to hang around
in the hope of another job.

It is work of endless variety. When participants
come for an interview they sometimes say, "You must
be tired hearing the same old thing." Every single participant I have met with has added a fresh insight, an-

other brick to the building, a building that they and I know will never be finished.

No intervention is value-free. I carry into an organisation my baggage of knowledge and ignorance, of values and received ideas. It is as well to get them out on the table before we deal with the Studies. They form the *Introduction* that follows.

Note: The book is hirsute with masculine pronouns. The number of female participants in the Studies was very small indeed. None of the chief executives was a woman. We have some grounds for hope that organisations of the future will reflect more accurately the reality of humankind: there is at least anecdotal evidence that women are breaking through.

Ivor Kenny
Woodview
University College
Dublin 4

December 1998

Chapter 1

INTRODUCTION: BACKGROUND AND VALUES

The true builder hates the lethargy of fortresses.
— René Char

FREEDOM

Management writers have produced a plethora of infantile books. They have also produced (as will I hope be clear from the endnotes in this book) some thoughtful writing. Because management theory is in its infancy — where economics was more than a hundred years ago — it has not yet developed guidelines, despite the optimism of authorities like the late Harold Koontz, my immediate predecessor as Chancellor of the International Academy of Management.[1]

Thoughtful writers can disagree wildly with each other. There is little dogma to be learned. Practising managers are still free to pick and choose whatever they fancy. Gurus flash across the sky. Some endure. Often those who endure write too much and talk too much (because the money is very good).

Exact knowledge is not available in management or, for that matter, in many of the sciences bearing on human behaviour — psychology, anthropology, sociology. In these developing disciplines, it is the approach or attitude that matters. That attitude is based on a conviction that a greater *degree* of knowledge is possible, that truths are being *developed* which can be applied to practical affairs. And, beyond the point where precision is possible, problems can be handled — as they are in medicine — in the temper and spirit of truth and with constant reference to experience, rather than in the half-light of custom and the limited data provided by individual empiricism.

We have, however, come a long way since Frederick Winslow Taylor (1856–1915), whose tomb at Germantown outside Philadelphia bears the simple phrase, "The Father of Scientific Management", or from his counterpart on this side of the Atlantic, Henri Fayol (1841–1925), whose paper, *Administration*, was presented in 1900 to the *Congrès des Mines et de la Métallurgie*.[2]

There is a marked movement in the literature from a directive, this-is-how-you-do-it approach to, if I may say so, a humbler, more holistic approach. And that is the ladder I have climbed.

The change both in the discipline and in myself is not a function merely of age, of mellowing. It is a function of continuous search, seasoned by experience. A young man will drive a car at 100 mph because he *knows* he is not going to die. An older man will slow down because he knows he is.

As well as the strategic explorations outlined below, I spend some time with individual chief executives. They may be concerned about the fact that next year looks like this year and this year looks like last: "I'm tired", they say, or "I'm fed up". We use the most powerful psychiatric tool known to man — a flip chart. I ask three questions on three successive evenings:

- What do you want?

- What's stopping you?

- What are you going to do?

"What do you want?" is the key. The flip chart gets covered with unsurprising things like love, respect, appreciation, power, a happy family, etc. But out of the predictable welter there usually comes a core need or value — and it is always about *freedom*. This is true for me also. In a master's thesis as long ago as 1954 I wrote,

> Freedom is not the power of doing what we like, but the right of being able to do what we ought. Freedom is essentially the faculty of choosing between the means which lead to a certain end: a person who has the ability to choose one thing among several others may be said to be free.[3]

Or, at that time quoting Lord Acton,

> By liberty I mean the assurance that every man shall be protected in doing what he believes his duty against the influence of authority and majority, custom and opinion.[4]

A survey quoted in Charles Handy's *Inside Organisations* showed that I shared my core value with many people.[5]

When people claim they love freedom, they can mean many things. In part, they are admiring the independence of freedom, the refusal to obey no matter what orders may be given. But they will often mean by freedom a fantasy in which all the frustrating restrictions under which they suffer have been removed. For while people may love freedom, they also love dependence. Those who come afresh to personal responsibility are likely to fear its risks and burdens. They like to take refuge in a function, to be told not only what to do but what they are. Only clear directions from outside can resolve stalemates in their personalities resulting from barely conscious conflicts. Such conflicts are personal problems which people may solve in a dogmatic way, by unquestioning adherence to a role, an organisation, a principle or a person. They may find a refuge in fundamentalism, the single-minded pursuit of highly simplified goals at the expense of thoughtful, open-minded, and compassionate concern for dissent and qualification. Fundamentalism offers the illusion of high-mindedness, a triumphant conviction of knowing one's own mind when others appear to be wavering.

Freedom is something quite different. Its essence lies in one person's will not being involuntarily subject to other human wills; in *my* will ruling over *my* actions, being checked only when it injures the indispensable requirements of life in society. Freedom is not a set of abstract things that we might do if we wished. It depends entirely on what we choose in action. Freedom is what we do, not what we may be allowed to do. Peter Schwartz says in *The Art of the Long View*:

> This book is about freedom. In western societies, people are ostensibly free, but they feel constrained by the unpredictability of events. Every year, every decade, we are surprised by social or technological upheavals that appear suddenly, surprisingly. How can people, businesses, and institutions plan for the future when they do not know what tomorrow will bring? A deep and realistic confidence is built on insight into the possible outcomes of our choices. In this unpredictable context, freedom is the ability to act both with confidence and a full knowledge of uncertainty.[6]

GOVERNMENT AND ENTERPRISE

In the 1970s and early 1980s, just before I began the Studies, government in Ireland had accumulated a literally crushing load of responsibilities — and the dependency, the unfreedom that those responsibilities generated. Government had reached what Louden Ryan called "disorganised over-complexity".[7] So long as it was dense and crowded, nothing was going to alter its proclivity to accumulate a stock of errors, nurse them to the point of infection, and waste time defending itself against deserved criticism. You could not fathom its objectives, accept its word or see where it was taking you. And yet, paradoxically, the public would go on demanding that it do more and more.

This is how bad things were in those years. Government expenditure had risen to two-thirds of Irish national output. In 1985, government spending was a third higher than government income. An example of the result was that the total revenue extracted from the populace in PAYE was not sufficient to pay even the interest on the national debt. In other words, those millions of pounds had been spent long ago. They were not available for investment, for growth, for jobs. They were merely keeping the bailiff from the door.

With people so fed up with government and compulsively demanding more, and with the political system compulsively responding, the ruling passion edged not towards the pursuit of liberty and enterprise but to a search for accountability, in a system where government was constantly extending its interventions and dispensations. T.K. Whitaker, when Secretary of the Department of Finance, described this phenomenon:

> Once a new service is undertaken it is practically impossible to get rid of it whether it continues to be necessary or not. It is strange how unfashionable, almost outmoded, is the idea of retrenchment. Not only is expenditure irreversible but the impossibility of putting a standstill on departmental activities inevitably forces it upwards. Who shall say how many ingenious ideas are born merely of a subconscious desire to justify a department's existence?[8]

This took us very near the rejection of the market system of plural choice.

Lest this appear apocalyptic, Dr Whitaker, by this time a senator, was moved to ask, "Who governs?"[9]

The eventual test of government is its ability to satisfy. That means its capacity to cope with the expectations, stresses and perceptions of its tangled constituencies. Its role is not merely to mind the shop — or to provide some sort of priesthood with the occasional strange inversion of ministers being invited to business dinners to tell businessmen how to run business. Government would simply have to shed unmanageable operational activities and bureaucracies to lighten its own bulk. If it was to do anything well, it would have to offload peripheral, as well as contentious, functions which were making a shambles of public management and satisfying not even the benefiting constituencies.

Underlying this conviction was, thankfully, a growing awareness of three disconcerting realities: (a) that the traditional hierarchical structure was inadequate to modern conditions; (b) that government knew no better than any of us and could make serious miscalculations that were paid for by all of us; and (c) that government was vulnerable to interest groups, in particular powerful public sector trade unions. Expectations of government became less ambitious:

> The main task of government is to set limits to inequality and to give individuals and households more rights against large organisations . . . The key here will be the struggle for opinion. There are some signs of a weakening hold of utopian thinking and the strengthening of a more empiricist approach to politics.[10]

My utterances on this subject attracted publicity. The book *Government and Enterprise in Ireland* was the centrepiece of an entire two-hour and more *Late Late Show*, Ireland's most popular television programme (and the longest running chat show in the world). It was on an icy February night when everybody was at home. (One of my critics on the show was Bertie Ahern, then a deputy, now Taoiseach. Bertie watched how the play was going before giving the ball a puck. Another critic was a Labour deputy, Michael D. Higgins. He got lost in his circumlocutions but had his revenge in an article he wrote for *Hot Press*, May 1986, entitled "Blessed Ivor and the Bean Baron's Ball".) The show's legendary host, Gay Byrne, asked me back to do a reprise of the programme. I refused. It was not so much my distrust of the medium as a growing repugnance at the personal publicity and the fact that I was becoming trapped, labelled a lightning rod for the (then) New Right.

If it was the error of twentieth-century state socialism to ascribe to governments a wisdom denied to any human institutions, it was the error of the New Right to suppose that market forces, if only they were left alone, would achieve a sort of natural co-ordination, which only government intervention disrupted.

New Rightists are neither angels nor devils. The New Right has its vice, and that vice is selfishness. New Rightists mutter, "Let me rest: I lie in possession." State socialism has its vice, and that vice is envy. State socialists growl, as in *Dr Faustus*, "Why shouldst thou sit, and I stand?"

The traditional conservative sees, instead of these counterpoised ideologies, the desperately humble task of endless improvisation, where one good is compromised for the sake of others, where a price has to be paid for everything, where a balance is sought among the necessary evils of human life and disaster is staved off for another day.

In any event, I decided to take the excellent advice of Sir Peter Medawar in the 1959 Reith Lectures: to stop wringing my hands over the human condition and to try instead to help remedy those things that were wholly remediable, to devote the rest of my life to what I knew best and loved — managers and organisations.

The problems of organisations are never wholly remediable but they are considerably more remediable than the problems of government. Underlying my writing about government was the enduring concern with freedom: antipathy to ordinary folk getting pushed around by, and becoming dependent on, powerful and ignorant forces. This same concern has informed my work with organisations.

We now have in Ireland several years of unprecedented national growth. In recent times, the increase in the number at work outstripped by a wide margin the increase over the previous 30 years. While this book was being written, in the year to May 1998, 95,000 new jobs were created. Unemployment dropped to a standardised rate of 7.2 per cent, compared with an EU average of 10.9 per cent. There is a shortage of skilled labour and net immigration (44,000 immigrants against 21,000 emigrants, April 1997–1998). To have jobs chasing people is a novel phenomenon in Ireland.

The country would not be true to its Celtic origins, however, if, underlying the Celtic Tiger, there was not a feeling of impermanence. There is an uncertain international scene. A price has been paid for economic growth. The public sector payroll, locked in rigid relativities, has steadily soaked up a disproportionate share of ever-increasing government expenditure. This phenomenon is by no means unique to Ireland.[11] That doughty trio, the police, the nurses and the teachers, have got, and will continue to get, pay increases beyond anything market sector workers have secured. One consequence is that national infrastructure has lagged well behind acceptable standards, despite significant EU funding. And many believe that too much of the growth has come from the volatile computer industry.

What these and other indicators boil down to is a country undergoing change in its values, its economy and its society, with no notion of an end-state because now there is no end-state. We have discussed long enough a world in constant flux. Now we are living through it.

A significant change in economic policy affecting the corporate sector is the collapse of the campaign against privatisation. Five short years ago, it was hard to have a rational discussion about the privatisation or, perhaps more accurately, the commercialisation, of state companies. The air was thick with rhetoric about the family silver, democratic rights, "public" ownership, exploitative capitalists and so drearily on to the (then) Irish Labour Party's irredentist "Not an inch!" All this at a time when we hoped dogma was dead.

A study by the World Bank of privatisation in Britain, Malaysia, Mexico and Chile found that in 11 out of 12 cases, there were big economic gains.[12] There is agreement that, as one study put it,

> Privatisation is a positive force in our society in that it increases efficiency and makes the companies more consumer conscious.[13]

Every solution creates its own problems.

> Privatisation offered an answer to problems concerning the effective control of state-owned industries, but it has created its own set of problems regarding the public regulation of major industries. As with other areas of economic policy, privatisation may come back to haunt the government.[14]

The argument against privatisation was never about dogma. The rhetoric was a smokescreen. The real agenda was about power. Nothing ever happens unless it is in somebody's interest for it to happen. Find out whose interest is at stake, ask *cui bono?*, and you will be close to understanding why things happen as they do. There were two power groups — the trade unions and the state — in an embrace that almost excluded the person who paid: the customer of the commercial state bodies. So, as John Redwood argued, "The most important thing of all [was] to re-establish a greater degree of sovereignty for the consumer."[15]

Now privatisation is given a qualified welcome by both the state and the trade unions — not remotely because of a conversion from ancient dogma, but simply because waves of competition from Brussels and the wider world have broken on the Irish shore. A commentator put it,

> It is certainly delightful to see public sector unions arguing, not over the iniquities of "casino capitalism" and "fat cats", but over their slice of the share-owning democracy through various share option schemes. Nothing is too good for the working classes.[16]

A 1998 survey put Ireland sixth, up from twelfth in 1997, among 46 countries, on "the extent to which government policies are conducive to competitiveness".[17]

STATE COMPANIES

Of the seven main Studies in this book, three are of state companies. State companies, compared with market sector companies, suffer unique strategic constraints.

The basic purpose of a business enterprise is to create a customer. If a business does not continue to create customers it cannot provide employment, pay its taxes or, ultimately, survive. Unless, of course, it is put on the life-support system of taxpayers' money or is a monopoly public utility which can charge what it likes.

The state is the worst possible sole shareholder a commercial enterprise could have:

- It has inconsistent and often irreconcilable objectives, making the enterprise very difficult to manage.

- It is control-oriented and risk-averse, and enterprise is about risk.

- It is interventionist, even in matters of detail.[18]

- It appoints boards, to put it delicately, of mixed quality, whose primary loyalty is to the minister who appoints them and not to the integrity of the enterprise.[19]

- It takes from even that board the power to reward, and, in some instances, to appoint, its chief executive.

- It imprisons the enterprise in iron-clad pay relativities.

- Lastly, because of its many competing priorities, it does not have the money or the will to support, as sole shareholder, the enterprise for which it bears sole responsibility.

Brian Joyce, Chairman of CIE, Ireland's most difficult state company, in a talk to the Chartered Institute of Transport, 17 November 1998, said,

> When I became non-executive chairman of CIE, I was none too pleased with the picture that emerged. The Group could best be described as having become a "creature" of successive departments and government ministers . . . It is not sur-

prising that governments, as ultimate shareholder,
would want to have a direct say in how commercial state companies carry out their respective re-
mits but not to a degree that cuts them off from
reality. There have been times when that vital relationship between CIE and its marketplace has
been seriously disconnected. The state of the infrastructure and rolling stock today is poor and reflects the "detached from reality" approach of
people in the civil service and government . . . You
will appreciate how difficult it might be to drive
one of our double-decker buses if someone elsewhere had control of the brakes, the accelerator
and the steering wheel.

It is a system that cannot work well.

The problems of managing commercial state bodies
lie in the mismatch between two distinct and different
systems: public and private. Until those differences are
recognised and separated, as is now happening (though
slowly), the difficulties with enterprise in the state sector will remain endemic.

Enterprise happens only where there is a high level of
personal, individual autonomy (and reward) and the
accountability that goes with that autonomy or freedom.
Where freedom is frustrated, enterprise is constrained.

At a conference of the Institute of Public Administration on 20 September 1990, the then Secretary of the
Department of Transport and Tourism, Donal
O'Mahony, while agreeing that state bodies must be
assured of freedom from interference in day-to-day operations, said that they could not enjoy total freedom
from government control for a number of reasons:

They are in public ownership, established or acquired by government with taxpayers' money.

They control a substantial proportion of total national resources and it is therefore vital that they be used in a way which will contribute to overall national objectives.

A number of them enjoy a monopoly or dominant position in strategic areas of the economy.

The large bodies have an important trend-setting effect, particularly in the area of pay and conditions of employment.

Some of them have a social dimension.

The objective of public enterprise control, therefore, is to see that public monies invested in state bodies are safeguarded and used to best effect, that state bodies conform generally to overall government policy and that the public sector operates efficiently and in a way that serves the best interests of the community. Policy must remain the prerogative of government, there must be an element of government control, and there must be a proper degree of public accountability.[20]

The language reflects the preoccupation of the bureaucracy: "control, safeguard, conform, prerogative, public accountability". It is not a system from which to expect a radical view. It is designed to manage marginal, not radical, change. Kevin Bonner, then Secretary of the Department of Enterprise and Employment, said recently,

Because of the extraordinary pace of change, old solutions become today's problems. The once vir-

tuous characteristics of stability and bureaucratic
control are now impediments . . .[21]

In business, managers are not radical by choice but by
necessity, because they are judged by results, not by
appearances. Radicalism requires absolute candour, a
refusal to change the subject when the conversation
gets uncomfortable. Above all, the radicalism of business requires intense effort to establish objectives: in
particular, the distinction between "want" objectives
("it would be nice if we can achieve them") and "must"
objectives ("it will be nasty if we can't"). It calls for
analytical staying power, the readiness to keep asking
"why", as the network of cause-and-effect proliferates.
Radicalism is the opposite of naïveté or wishful thinking. It is the art of the necessary.

Radicalism in this sense is dismissed by most experienced politicians as too "theoretical". The idea that
certain problems that have been long regarded as insoluble must nevertheless be solved if greater evils are
to be avoided makes them uneasy. They quote examples of how the unexpected has upset the best-laid
plans. Like managers in the 1960s, resisting the en-
croachment of professionalism, politicians insist that
their business is different. Unfortunately for state enterprise, they are right.

There is little sense of system, of dynamic processes,
despite the fact that all significant problems for government are systems problems. Solutions are often discussed before there is agreement about the nature of
the problem. Papers prepared by departments are often

accepted without question as the only menu from which options can be ordered. Ministers tend to present their views, from analysis to prescription, in set speeches one by one. Even major objectives are never developed into hierarchies or networks of sub-objectives. This makes it difficult to begin, because no one has worked out where the beginning is.

Perhaps most importantly, the much-used word "strategy" is not understood as the step-by-step removal of removable constraints (administrative, political, economic) so as to make an insoluble problem soluble. There is a confusion between winning today's battles, which is one thing, and making tomorrow's battles winnable, which is quite another. Thus the first question asked is "How are we going to solve this problem?" when it should be, "Why is this problem at present insoluble?"

If you put all these things together and add the time pressures on ministers, it is not difficult to see that the process all too often degenerates into the trading of departmental views, stockpiled from previous years. Fergus Finlay wrote recently:

> . . . the primary skill a great politician needs . . . is a talent for crisis management. The time and space to develop visions and dreams, to work out how to change society for the better, are almost never given to a politician in government . . . the daily grind of government can wear them down.[22]

There must be at least as much talent in the public sector as there is in the private sector. It is simply not focused either on the strategic view or on day-to-day efficiency. The public service tends to control administrative and financial management in detail by excessively strong, central procedures. Much of what constitutes government policy does not provide a stable sense of direction for actually getting the work done, as policy does in well-managed businesses. Contact between the minister's office and the operating manager is usually about crises and infrequently about what strategies are appropriate to a changing marketplace. In other words, state companies operate in a *culture* significantly different from the culture of private enterprise.

CULTURE

Culture gives an organisation shared values and norms. It can be a force for good: for example, in building commitment and team spirit. It can also be inhibiting: for example, in causing managers to see the world through the same filter. What appears as a rational strategy is frequently culture-laden. Since there is never a "right" strategy, this may not matter much and a successful organisation's momentum may be sufficient to carry it over the occasional pothole. But it has inherent dangers.

Organisations go through periods when strategies appear to be developed incrementally. Strategic decisions build upon one another in small steps, following a path in which history plays an important part in shaping the future. More fundamental shifts in strategy occur infrequently as major readjustments take place.

Managers consciously pursue an incremental approach to managing complexity: they are aware that it is not possible to "know" about all the influences that could conceivably affect the future of the organisation. They are also aware that the organisation is a political entity in which trade-offs between different groups are inevitable. It is never possible to arrive at an optimal goal or an optimal strategy. Strategies are compromises that allow the organisation to go forward. To cope with compromise, strategies must be developed in stages, carrying the members of the organisation with them.

While individual managers may hold varying beliefs about the world, there is usually an identifiable core set of beliefs held fairly commonly.

This set of beliefs is taken for granted and not problematic. It may be more easily perceived by those outside the organisation than by those inside. Liam Gorman noted:

> Deeper layers of culture are responsible for managers' tendencies to see the world, people, actions and events in a certain way. They frequently come to believe that their perceptions and actions are based on incontrovertible "truths".[23]

This can encourage a homogeneous approach to the interpretation of complexity: the confusing signals that the organisation faces are made sense of, filtered, in terms of this set of beliefs. Moreover, since the culture evolved over time and is reinforced through the history and success of the organisation, it also provides a repertoire of responses: it is both a device for interpretation and a formula for action. The strategies grow out of this set of beliefs.

Managers may recognise changes going on around them, inside or outside the organisation, but this does not mean that they see those changes as directly relevant. Relevance is determined, not by the competitive environment, but by the set of beliefs: if outside stimuli can be explained within the set of beliefs, then that becomes "the reality" for action by the organisation. What you see depends on where you stand.

The set of beliefs is protected by symbols, myths and rituals which legitimise it: routines which programme the way members of the organisation respond to given situations, which delineate "the way we do things here". Those with the greatest power may derive their power partly from their association with the set of beliefs, which serve to reduce uncertainty, enhance their status and link them to the success of the organisation. You cannot separate a set of beliefs from what an organisation actually does: they are strung together in a cultural web.

It is therefore difficult to challenge or change the set of beliefs unless these changes are evolutionary or incremental. Challenges are likely to be disturbing because they attack those beliefs that are central to a manager's life.

Challenges are not a matter of intellectual debate or cool analysis. This is an important distinction. An objective, analytical assessment of an organisation can yield knowledge but it is not knowledge which managers will interpret intellectually and objectively and assimilate in such a way as to change strategy. Such analyses typically evoke a political or emotional rather than an intellectual response. To believe that strategic change can come about as a result of analysis and evaluation would be to fall into a reigning Irish error: thinking that we had solved a problem because we had described it.

Even when there are changes in the organisation's environment which conflict with the beliefs, there is unlikely to be a wholesale change in the beliefs. The conflict will be resolved by those who can exercise the greatest degree of power. Vijay Sathe argues that:

> The challenge for leaders is to harness culture's benefits while remaining alert to the dangers of perpetuating a culture that is out of tune with the needs of business, the organisation and its members. Enlightened leadership can avoid cultural blind spots by accommodating selective nonconformity in their organisations, and by themselves deviating from culture when the situation calls for it.[24]

If we look at strategic management this way, the phenomenon of incremental strategic development in organisations is explained rather differently. Instead of being a logical testing out of strategies in action, we see the process as a response that is internally constructed rather than objectively understood. In these circumstances it is likely that, over time, the phenomenon of strategic drift may occur: that is, gradually, probably imperceptibly, the strategy of the organisation may become less in tune with its environment or markets. This can take time and quite likely will not be discerned by managers until the drift becomes so marked that decline sets in. It is then that more fundamental changes in strategy are likely.

Then there is a need to unfreeze the set of beliefs. Outsiders — that is, individuals with little or no loyalty to the beliefs — may play a vital role in questioning that which is taken for granted.

However, outsiders come into organisations with their own agendas. They tend not to focus on the question of where the organisation came from, how its structures and mores developed, and what implications aetiology may have for process and performance. They accept as a given the organisational context they enter. But organisations do have memories, they do learn and, occasionally, unlearn. Snapshots tend to underestimate seriously the significance of organisational memories and learning abilities.

More dynamic perspectives on organisations are badly needed. Outsiders, if their interventions are to be of enduring value, must painstakingly build a relationship that enables them to maintain independence, integrity, outsidedness, while being given the time and freedom to seek causes, not effects.

The extent to which an outsider's new perspectives can be developed into a different strategy is likely to depend on the extent to which managers within the organisation feel confident enough about the need for change to become constructively critical of their own history and its dominant beliefs.

"Strategic drift" has been defined as an organisation's becoming less in tune with its environment or markets. Mixed in with it, but identifiably separate, is another, more subtle, form of drift, which might be called "organisational (or ideological) drift".

THE CHIEF EXECUTIVE

Chief executives are (or should be) the walking embodiment of the ideals (or ideology) of their organisations. If they are to live in any comfort, they must foster an atmosphere in which their unique ideas can be understood and reinforced. In other words, this informal, unwritten side of the organisation must be developed along with the formal structure and process. Without special attention, it will tend to develop independently of formal structures and intentions, to drift off on its own. The term "organisational drift" means the gap between the chief executive's ideals and intentions and the organisation as experienced.

Strategic drift is caused by uncertainty about *where* an organisation is going. *Organisational* drift is about *how* it is going (or not going) there. Strategic drift is about unclear direction. Organisational drift is about unclear standards — the most obvious of which is a diminution in the concern for quality, usually at the expense of expediency. And quality is not just about what the customer gets, but is also the quality of the processes within the organisation.

Business thrives on unity of command. There are normally no power bases independent of the chief executive. Authority flows from the shareholder to the board of directors to the chief executive and from there to other executives. Anyone who seeks to create a power base independent of the chief executive, who creates a barony within a princely state, can do so only because the chief executive is weak.

I used to believe that a good manager could manage anything. (So did Harold Geneen of IT&T — a corporation known to his subordinates as International This and That.) Perhaps there are people with superb technical and social skills who, given time and a painful learning process, can master an environment different from that in which they were brought up. They would certainly be the exception and their absorption by a new organisation would have been at a high price.

A new leader from outside will often feel a compulsion to rush in like the tide and make changes. However, when the tide recedes, the old rocks are still sticking up. The culture — the sedimented attitudes and behaviour patterns in the firm — will not have altered at all. Worse, the organisation, like an oyster, will have learned to protect itself from this intrusion by laying down layers through which, try as they may, new chief executives may never penetrate.

Chief executives who enjoy charismatic gifts might copy Luther and nail their ideals to the door: "All who agree, get in; all who don't, get out". This is a course of considerable appeal, but they must be sure the best remain.

The military historian, B.H. Liddell-Hart, in one of his last books, *Why Don't We Learn From History?* (1969), analysed what he called The Fallacy of Compulsion:

> We learn from history that the compulsory principle always breaks down in practice. It is practicable to *prevent* men doing something; moreover that principle of restraint, or regulation, is essentially justifiable insofar as its application is needed to check interference with others' freedom. But it is not, in reality, possible to *make* men do something without risking more than is gained from the compelled effort. The method may appear practicable, because it often works when applied to those who are merely hesitant. When applied to those who are definitely unwilling it fails, however, because it generates friction and fosters subtle forms of evasion that spoil the effect which is sought. The test of whether a principle works is to be found in the product.

Efficiency, as I mentioned in the *Preface*, springs from enthusiasm — because this alone can develop a dynamic impulse. Enthusiasm is incompatible with compulsion — because it is essentially spontaneous. Compulsion is thus bound to deaden enthusiasm — because it dries up the source.

True consent can be gained only by persuasion. Enduring enthusiasm can be gained only by participation. When an impatient and powerful chief executive finds his organisation drifting away from him, he may be attracted to compulsion. This is like responding to a

complex social problem by saying, "There ought to be a
law about it". But the law's roots are in sanctions and
make it too rough an instrument for the kind of management we need today. Laws are there to stop the bad
guys. No one expects managers to be philosophers, on
the one hand; but, on the other, the impulsion to activity, the reduction of complexity to childish slogans, the
"Let-me-have-it-on-one-sheet-of-paper" syndrome, can
suppress the reality of the world and lead to surprises,
many of them unpleasant. There is nothing more
frightening than ignorance in motion.[25] What we are
looking for are ways to mobilise the energies of good
guys.

CONSENSUS MANAGEMENT

The informal processes which lead to organisational
drift are too vaguely understood to be *managed* effectively. They may, indeed, be the most important strategic problems confronting managers in the next decades:
discovery of new arrangements, organisational forms,
relationships and processes which can persuade people
at work to volunteer their minds and energies to purposes they consider worthwhile. Peter Drucker wrote in
The Age of Discontinuity: "Management is simple but not
easy. The simple part is knowing what to do. The part
that is not easy is getting others to do it."[26]

We do not know all we need to know about how we
reconcile motivational needs with the needs of purposeful organisations, but we know enough to be getting on with. We certainly know that, however

attractive it may seem, autocracy does not work over the long term. We know that, in innovative organisations, there will be a need for greater involvement with the job as an experience in itself, instead of as a burden tolerated for future promotion or reward. We know that there will be a desire for greater collegiality, that there will be an increase in assertiveness and a demand for supervision to demonstrate competence and co-operation, rather than to depend on hierarchic authority. This, in the literature, is old hat. In management practice, in dealing with organisational drift, we are still a long way from it, never mind pushing out to Charles Handy's new horizons.

It requires constant vigilance to steer successfully between the Scylla of autocracy, pandering to base instincts and causing dependence, and the Charybdis of consensus management, the lowest common denominator of agreement, drowning process in lethargy.

SOME MANAGEMENT MYTHS

Once upon a time, management was PLOC — Planning, Leading, Organising and Controlling. One of the benefits of these four pillars of wisdom was that they neatly formed a two-day seminar I launched in 1962 on the unsuspecting (and tolerant) managers of Ireland. PLOC was the great legacy of Henri Fayol (*q.v.*).[27] In 1916, management was in dire need of scientific credibility. To describe it in rational PLOC terms was to lend it a veneer of respectability.

During the 1960s, however, the myth of the manager as rational information-handler and decision-maker was exploded. Managers, in common with a lot of other people, do not always live in reality. In an Irish poll (1987), 52 per cent of the chief executives interviewed believed the economy would decline, while 36 per cent thought that it would improve. When, however, they were asked how their own companies would fare, the percentages were almost exactly reversed: 53 per cent thought their own companies would do better, while only 33 per cent thought they would decline.[28]

There is more than an echo here of the work done by the late Paddy Dillon-Malone.[29] He found that what is perceived at the general level is not always related back to the individual, who tends to see himself as an exception to the rule. Many Irish firms, faced with free trade, believed they themselves would survive in the 1970s. The others would go to the wall. They were, unfortunately, wrong. This euphoria is like the bravado with which soldiers go into battle, knowing that some of them are going to be killed, but none of them believing it will be themselves.

Managers make it more difficult by continuing to subscribe to two enduring myths. A first myth is: "There is light at the end of the tunnel." This is the Blue Lagoon Syndrome — the belief that when we have sorted out present difficulties we shall find a tranquil haven. In their hearts, managers know this is a myth, but it is part of what keeps them going. It is dangerous only if it is allowed unduly to influence decisions. In workshops in Western countries, in China and in the erstwhile Soviet Union, I made a point of asking managers the penetrating question, "How's business?" The answer invariably was, across those different cultures, "Next year is going to be difficult, but after that we should be all right."

The longer I work with managers, the more I am impressed with their inability to forecast the future. For a year ahead, the headlamps can pick out some forms. After that it is murk.

The second popular myth is: "We're all in this together." Organisations create dependency relationships. Dependency relationships are barriers to the truth. Barriers are necessary things in everyday living. Otherwise we could drive on the left- or right-hand side of the road whenever the whim took us. You don't visit a friend in hospital and say, "My God, you look bloody awful!" You don't say to a colleague who has resigned, "Great! That opens the way for me." You don't say to your boss, "I think that's the most idiotic idea I've ever heard."

White lies, maybe. They can shade dangerously into grey where there are dependency relationships, barriers, as there can be in friendships, in families — and in work organisations.

DEPENDENCY

People in organisations withhold from one another what they think and feel about what goes on. They are never completely frank about the direction the organisation is going in, about the pressures from competing enterprises, about the way decisions are made or the style of leadership, about the way resources are allocated or who are the favourite sons.

People worry about what their boss thinks of them. They worry about their peers with whom they compete for the favour of a common superior. They worry about their subordinates, younger and more recently educated, whose acquired knowledge of the organisation may soon rival their own.

Consequently, they never fully open up. Part of their inner truth they communicate, part they conceal, and part is the opposite of their real thoughts and feelings. No organisation is free from this disease. Most people, when they hear of it, are surprised at its universality — they think it affects only them. It is the major contributor to organisations' not knowing where they stand. It causes defensiveness and dependencies that are barriers to living in the real world.

Working once in Australia, I asked a chief executive what he did. He paused and said, "I build a team". When I asked his subordinates what they did, they said, "We work for Joe".

Melvin Dalton gave us an insight into the machinations which take up a manager's time. He helped us appreciate the managerial underlife of organisations in which informal arrangements replace, impede and combine with official procedures. The successful managers were those most at ease in this ambiguous system.

Persons able to deal with confusion came to the fore as leaders, with or without the official title. They became the nucleus of cliques that work as interlocking action centres and as bridges between official and unofficial purposes.[30]

So much for PLOC. Dalton was saying that informal ad hoc practices were the lubricant of working organisations and the preservers of managerial sanity. Henry Mintzberg gave an added twist by asserting that chaos was the work of managers, that management work was characterised by "brevity, variety and fragmentation".[31] (He stopped before Hobbes's "nasty, brutish and short".)

John Kotter has sold the idea of managerial work as a kind of camouflaged planning.[32] He maintains that managers plan implicitly, on their feet, and that reactive behaviour is, in fact, an opportunistic way of achieving much in a short time. Disjointed reactions are not a sign of impulsiveness but a means of rapidly scanning a range of problems.

The pendulum has swung to its limit, with Kotter maintaining that management involves no identifiable reflection, since reflection is incorporated into the action itself.

THE MANAGEMENT OF PARADOX: A QUESTION OF SYNTHESIS

Strategy is a thoughtful analysis of a business as a basis for setting attainable goals. A good strategy does not

lock you into a simplistic analysis of complex realities.
Mintzberg wrote:

> Strategy-making is an immensely complex process
> involving the most sophisticated, subtle, and at
> times subconscious of human cognitive and social
> processes. We know that it must draw on all kinds
> of informational inputs, many of them non-
> quantifiable and accessible only to strategists who
> are connected to the details rather than detached
> from them. We know that the dynamics of the
> context have repeatedly defied any efforts to force
> the process into a pre-determined schedule or onto
> a pre-determined track. Strategies inevitably ex-
> hibit some emergent qualities, and even when
> largely deliberate, often appear less formally
> planned than informally visionary . . . We know
> that the process requires insight, creativity, and
> synthesis, the very things that formalisation dis-
> courages.[33]

It is a continuous process: choosing goals, action plans,
implementing, and correcting for errors and surprises.
It is hard work. It needs time to do the analysis and
then the determination to take the tough decisions
about products and people that the analysis throws up.
It means writing thoughtful things down — something
to which managers seem to have an abiding aversion,
so strong that many quit at the first obstacle, or at the
first possibility of a flight to action, the opiate of the
manager.

The plain, blunt manager, armed with a plain, simple plan, can be an attractive figure. He sums up his

fundamentalist philosophy in one — or perhaps two — telling phrases (which he will have borrowed).

By contrast, the effective manager is adept at handling complexity. He thinks in a complex way. He wheels and deals, negotiates, trades off, finds his subtle way through a multitude of variables. He would not be overly moved by 510 pages of Ansoff.[34] He might, however, find useful echoes in Robert M. Pirsig's *Zen and the Art of Motorcycle Maintenance*, which begins

> And what is good, Phaedrus,
> And what is not good —
> Need we ask anyone to tell us these things?[35]

Hear what Pirsig has to say about *stuckness*:

> A screw sticks, for example, on a side cover assembly of your motorcycle. You check the manual to see if there might be any special cause for this screw to come off so hard, but all it says is "Remove side cover plate" in that wonderful terse technical style that never tells you what you want to know.
>
> The book's no good to you now. Neither is scientific reason. You don't need any scientific experiments to find out what's wrong. It's obvious what's wrong. What you need is a hypothesis for how you're going to get that slotless screw out of there and scientific method doesn't provide any of these hypotheses. It operates only after they're around.
>
> Traditional scientific method has always been, at the very best, 20/20 hindsight. It's good for seeing where you've been. It's good for testing the truth

of what you think you know, but it can't tell you
where you *ought* to go, unless where you ought to
go is a continuation of where you were going in
the past. Creativity, originality, inventiveness, intuition, imagination — "unstuckness", in other
words — are completely outside its domain.

Management is practice. There are few blueprints, few
grand plans. There are no solutions that can be trans-
ferred at a gulp from one bit of experience to another.
That is not to say that nothing is fixed, that there are no
guidelines, that we can make everything up as we go
along.

It is to say that correction is contingent on the circumstances of the time, the constraints and opportunities, the culture or sedimented attitudes of the people
we have to work with. This is where Pirsig's quality of
"unstuckness" comes in: creativity, originality, inventiveness, intuition and imagination, qualities that are
hard to measure — and science depends on the ability
to measure.

That benign philosopher, E.F. Schumacher, who first
said "Small is beautiful", said,

> Some people always tend to clamour for a final
> solution, as if in life there could ever be a final so-
> lution other than death. For constructive work, the
> principal task is always the restoration of some
> kind of balance.[36]

And, as the Book of Common Prayer says, we should avoid "the two extremes, of too much stiffness in refusing, and too much easiness in admitting any variation".

Management is about balance, about freedom *and* order. Balance means the acceptance of paradox. Some know this. Uncertainty, the necessity of imperfect choice, makes others uneasy. Some like fixed things. If pushed, they may raise them to the level of "principles". "Sticking to our principles" is about as sensible as being against the use of electricity if it is merely an unwillingness to face uncertainty or paradox. Compromise is not a heroic word. It has none of the rock-like certainty of fundamentalism (*q.v*), of "No surrender!"

Few things are black and white, clear-cut, either/or, so that we have to manage in a way that *accepts the existence of contradictory phenomena without trying to resolve them.*

Some years ago I brought the French and Irish board members of the Smurfit Paribas Bank off for a day to answer the question, "What kind of bank do you want?" On one flip chart, we wrote things like: warm, friendly, welcoming, relaxed, non-hierarchical. On another we wrote: entrepreneurial, quick-moving, decisive and so on. Which did they choose? Both.

Evans and Doz have presented a daunting list of false dichotomies:[37]

Managing today's assets/rents	Building tomorrow's assets/rents
Customer orientation	Being ahead of the customer
Short term	Long term
Competition	Partnership
Low cost	High value-added
Speed of responsiveness	Care in implementation
Differentiation	Integration
Centralisation	Decentralisation
Unit performance	Corporate integration
Loose	Tight
Opportunistic	Planned
Entrepreneur	Control
Change	Continuity
"Loyalty"	"Layoffs"
"Hardware"	"Software"
Individual accountability	Team responsibility
Rewarding individuals	Rewarding teams
Professional	Generalist
Technical logic	Business logic
Top down	Bottom up
Tolerance	Forthrightness
Taking risks	Avoiding failures
Task orientation	People orientation
Analysis	Intuition

Michael Smurfit, head of the Jefferson Smurfit Group, a world leader in its industry, describes his strategy:

> I believe that logical opportunism is one way of
> approaching the complex task of management
> which, simply put, means being creative while at
> the same time keeping a strong grip on the key
> day-to-day elements of the business, including fi-
> nancial controls.[38]

Logic (thought) and opportunism (action) are not *oppo-
sites*. We need the "Let's go!" of leadership. We also
need the "Hold on a minute" of cool advice. Just as we
need both patience and impatience.

Ambiguity (*ambi-*, both ways, *agere*, to drive) has two
important things to offer managers. First, it is useful in
thinking about how we communicate with others. Second, it provides a way of legitimising the loose rein that
a manager permits in situations where agreement
needs time, or where further insight is needed before
decisive action can be taken.

Many managers are under fierce day-to-day pressure merely to survive. Macho managers go like a bull
at a gate. They may succeed once. The second time, the
gate has been reinforced and all they get is a sore head.
The better manager is adept at handling complexity
and its consequent ambiguity.

Our drive for the explicit stems from the notion that
it's a matter of honour to get all the cards out on the
table. There is also the notion that, no matter how much
it hurts, full frontal exposure is good for you: the sign
of a good manager is his or her ability to give and take
negative feedback. No doubt there is merit in this con-
ventional wisdom. But the true state of things often lies
between the mythology of our management lore and

our human foibles. It *is* good to get the facts and to know where you stand. But it's also human to feel threatened when you are vulnerable.

Delivering yourself of the need to "speak the truth" often unmasks a self-serving sense of brute integrity. "Clearing the air" can be more helpful to the clearer than to those starkly revealed. The issue of brute integrity is not just an outcome of a certain cultural tendency to speak plainly and bluntly. Simplistic confrontation — a kind of *High Noon* shoot-out — is mixed up with notions of strength. Unfortunately, shoot-outs work best when the other guy dies. When you have to continue to work with him, such macho confrontations tend to complicate life: he will be waiting in the long grass.

By contrast, ambiguity, in reference to sensitivity and feelings, is seen as weakness. Sensitivity does not rule out toughness when toughness is needed. It does not mean taking the easy way out — the corruption of management. It does not mean that there will never be confrontations best dealt with by the effective use of two syllables. But we should not confuse heroics with effectiveness. Are brute integrity and explicit communication worth the price of the listener's trust, goodwill, open-mindedness and receptivity to change?

Management by decree has a part to play in organisations, particularly in emergencies. But, more often than not, a sudden lurch to a new order will evoke informal resistance that works with enduring effectiveness.

Our notions of leadership embrace a number of images: strength, firmness, determination and clarity of vision. We like to think of leaders as lonely figures capable of decisive action in the face of adversity. These assumptions − for that is what they are − act as fortresses keeping some things in and other things out of our awareness.

Approaching things purposively, defining problems crisply and identifying explicitly our objectives are desirable, but not necessarily sufficient, qualities with which to manage all problems skilfully. We might also bear in mind that a macho view of the world lessens our sensitivity and skills. And such an insight may enable us to avoid using a sledgehammer when a feather will do. But keep the hammer handy lest we fall back into the trap of false dichotomies.

It *is* a question of balance between freedom and order. But it is even more a question of fusion or *synthesis*. Richard Pascale wrote:

> Neither "planned" nor "opportunistic" *extremes* alone provide the long-term answer. Organisations need both. The answer lies in a "dynamic synthesis" − not a compromise or mathematical halfway house of strategic and opportunistic tendencies, but a *paradoxical embrace* that contains both poles.[39]

The UCD crest gets the synthesis nicely: *Ad astra* − reach for the stars, for excellence; and *Comhthrom Féinne* − with fairness to everyone.

Notes

1. "We may be moving more than people think towards a unified and practical theory of management." Harold Koontz (1980), "The Management Theory Jungle Revisited", *Academy of Management Review*, Vol. 5, No. 2, p. 175.

2. Henry Fayol (1900), "Administration Industrielle et Générale — Prévoyance, Organisation, Coordination, Contrôle", *Bulletin de la Societé de l'Industrie Minérale*. Republished in book form, Paris: Dunod, 1925.

3. Ivor Kenny (1954), *Church and State in Western Europe*, M.A. Dissertation.

4. J.N. Figgis and R.V. Laurence (eds.) (1907), *Lord John Acton: The History of Freedom and Other Essays*, London: Macmillan, pp. 3–4.

5. Charles Handy (1990), *Inside Organisations*, London: BBC Books, p. 28.

6. Peter Schwartz (1991), *The Art of the Long View*, London: Century Business, p. 3.

7. Louden Ryan (1982), "Prospects for the '80s", *The Economic and Social State of the Nation*, Dublin: Economic and Social Research Institute, p. 85.

8. T.K. Whitaker, quoted in: Ronan Fanning (1978), *The Irish Department of Finance 1922–58*, Dublin: Institute of Public Administration, p. 578.

9. *Business and Finance*, 18 December 1980.

10. Nick Bosanquet (1983), *After the New Right*, London: Heinemann, pp. 203–4.

11. "If the public sector could talk it would say 'pay me first' . . . What existed was not a smooth system of medium-term planning, but a succession of great lunges — precipitous spending cuts and increases, especially in capital spending — interspersed with a gradual creep in public spending that went by default . . . the record of the last seven years is worthy of Colonel Blimp's best mock salute, a not quite describable combina-

tion of utter dismay and grudging admiration." Hugh Heclo and Aaron Wildavsky (1981), *The Private Government of Public Money*, London: Macmillan, pp. xxviii-l.

12. "Privatisation", *The Economist*, 21 August 1993, p. 18.

13. Abbass F. Alkhafaji (1993), "Privatisation: an Overview", *Journal of Organisational Change Management*, Vol. 6, No. 3, p. 40.

14. David Parker and Steve Martin (1993), "Testing Time for Privatisation", *Management Today*, August, p. 47.

15. John Redwood (1980), *Public Enterprise in Crisis: the Future for the Nationalised Industries*, Oxford: Basil Blackwell, p. 202.

16. Aidan Kane, "Privatisation: the Right Policy, the Wrong Reasons", *The Sunday Business Post*, 9 August 1998, p. 23.

17. Stéphane Garelli (ed.) (1998), *The World Competitiveness Yearbook, 1998*, Lausanne: IMD, p. 26.

18. "The general suspicion of such intervention became another plank in the argument in favour of privatisation. The transfer of ownership from public to private hands can also be an opportunity for the authorities to demonstrate in a credible manner that they will no longer interfere in the day-to-day running of the business in favour of interests unrelated to the firm." *Conjoncture* (1995), Paris: Banque Paribas, February, No. 2, p. 19.

19. "You might as well be telling the cat not to drink milk as trying to discourage ministers from putting on boards some of their inadequately experienced political friends." Michael Dargan (former head of Aer Lingus), quoted in: Ivor Kenny (1987), *In Good Company*, Dublin: Gill and Macmillan, pp. 117–8.

20. Donal O'Mahony's remarks were incorporated, somewhat diluted, as part of *Employment through Enterprise: the Response of the Government to the Moriarty Task Force and the Implementation of the Culliton Report* (1993), Dublin: The Stationery Office, p. 35.

21. Kevin Bonner, Secretary, Department of Enterprise and Employment (1995), "Government and Business — Antagonists or Partners?" Address to Irish Management Institute Conference, 31 March.

22. Fergus Finlay (1998), *Snakes & Ladders*, Dublin: New Island Books, p. 14.

23. Liam Gorman (1989), "Corporate Culture", *Management Decision*, Vol. 27, No. 1, p. 18. See also: Craig C. Lundberg (1990), "Surfacing Organisational Culture", *Journal of Managerial Psychology*, Vol. 5, No. 4, pp. 19–26.

24. Vijay Sathe (1983), "Implications of Corporate Culture: a Manager's Guide to Action", *Organisational Dynamics*, Autumn, p. 22.

25. Reg Revans, quoted in: Ivor Kenny (1988), *Management and Mythology*, Centenary Address to the Institute of Chartered Accountants, April.

26. Peter F. Drucker (1969), *The Age of Discontinuity: Guidelines to Our Changing Society*, London: Heinemann. See pp. 268-290.

27. *Op. cit.*

28. *Business and Finance*, 27 August – 3 September 1987.

29. Patrick Dillon-Malone (1970), *An Analysis of Marketing*, Dublin: Irish Management Institute.

30. Melvin Dalton (1959), *Men Who Manage*, New York: Wiley, p. 294.

31. Henry Mintzberg (1973), *The Nature of Managerial Work*, New York: Harper & Row, p. 162.

32. John Kotter (1986), *The General Managers*, New York: The Free Press, *passim*.

33. Henry Mintzberg (1994), *The Rise and Fall of Strategic Planning*, London: Prentice Hall, p. 227.

34. H. Igor Ansoff (1984), *Implementing Strategic Management*, Englewood Cliffs, NJ: Prentice Hall.

35. Robert M. Pirsig (1983), *Zen and the Art of Motor Cycle Maintenance*, Corgi Books, pp. 272-3.

36. E.F. Schumacher (1973), *Small is Beautiful*, London: Blond & Briggs Ltd., p. 19.

37. P. Evans and Y. Doz (1989), "The Dualist Organization", in Evans and Doz, *Human Resource Management in International Firms: Change, Globalization, Innovation*, London: Macmillan. See also: P. Thygesen Poulsen (1993), "The Paradoxes of Success", *LEGO — en virksomhed og dens sjael*, Copenhagen: Schultz.

"• To be able to build a close relationship with one's staff . . . *and to keep a subtle distance.*

• To be able to lead . . . *and to hold oneself in the background.*

• To trust one's staff . . . *and to keep an eye on what is happening.*

• To be tolerant . . . *and to know how you want things to function.*

• To keep the goals of one's own department in mind . . . *and at the same time to be loyal to the whole firm.*

• To do a good job of planning your own time . . . *and to be flexible with your schedule.*

• To express freely your own views . . . *and to be diplomatic.*

• To be a visionary . . . *and to keep one's feet on the ground.*

• To try to win consensus . . . *and to be able to cut through.*

• To be dynamic . . . *and to be reflective.*

• To be sure of yourself . . . *and to be humble.*"

38. Michael W.J. Smurfit (n.d.), *The International Growth of an Irish Enterprise*, The Dillon-Malone Lecture, Dublin: Jefferson Smurfit Group PLC, p. 4.

39. Richard Pascale (1993), *Managing on the Edge: How Successful Companies Use Conflict to Stay Ahead*, London: Penguin Books, p. 53.

Chapter 2

THE STUDIES: PURPOSE AND METHOD

*People are generally better persuaded by the reasons
they have themselves discovered than by those which
have come into the mind of others.*
— Blaise Pascal

FIVE SIMPLE PREMISES

The purpose of the Studies, on which most of this book
is based, is to free up an organisation so that it knows
itself better and gets a firmer grip on its future through
having a clear, shared view of where it is going and
why.

The Studies rest on five simple premises:

First, all organisations create dependency relationships and dependency relationships inhibit truth, the
understanding of reality. All successful organisations
tend to reinforce their own basic beliefs, to believe their
own propaganda.

Second, the people who work in an organisation
know more about it than any outsider: they know it in
their bones. There is a crucial difference between the
prescriptive style adopted by accountants or lawyers

and the style adopted in the Studies. The difference was
described by Stephen Swartz:

> Consider the difference between the professions
> that require the acquisition and transfer of technical
> expertise (such as accounting and the law) and the
> professions that place more emphasis on education
> and personal development (such as applied behav-
> ioural science and family psychology). The former
> tend to assume that the client has accurately de-
> scribed the problem and that the job of the expert is
> to provide the correct answer. These professions
> have a fundamentally prescriptive orientation. The
> objective is to help by conveying precise technical
> knowledge to the client. For these professionals am-
> biguity is the enemy. By contrast, psychologists are
> more interested in creating conditions that enhance
> the capability of clients to help themselves. The
> primary emphasis is on change through insight and
> education. For psychologists, ambiguity may be
> welcomed as an opportunity to change a client's
> pre-conceived views on a given issue.[1]

Third, the only way organisations can be helped to un-
cover that knowledge is to use a trusted outsider (not,
in this instance, a psychologist, *pace* Swartz) who brings
a different, objective perspective. Organisations cannot
do it by themselves, from inside. (That is why internal
group planning exercises or strengths-and-weaknesses
analyses leave a lingering sense of incompleteness.)

Fourth, the most effective way to explore the organisation is to identify how it is experienced by individuals:

> Solutions that concentrate on groups . . . fail to take
> into account the real nature of employment sys-

tems. People are not employed in groups. They are employed individually, and their employment contracts — real or implied — are individual. Group members may insist in moments of great *esprit de corps* that the group as such is the author of some particular accomplishment, but once the work is completed, the members of the group look for individual recognition and individual progression in their careers. And it is not groups but individuals whom the company will hold accountable. The only true group is the board of directors, with its corporate liability. None of the group-oriented panaceas face this issue of accountability. All the theorists refer to group authority, group decisions and group consensus, none of them to group accountability. Indeed, they avoid the issue of accountability altogether, for to hold a group accountable, the employment contract would have to be with the group, not with the individuals, and companies simply do not employ groups as such.[2]

Pope put it more succinctly: "The proper study of mankind is man."

Finally, the only people who carry out recommendations with any energy are the people who make them. That is why many finger-wagging consultants' reports suffer death in the drawer. According to Robert O. Metzger:

> There are too many consultants, or firms professing to be consultants, which find it easier to sell insecure clients what they want, say, top-down control systems, than what they need. For the moment, it is still easier to sell and reap fees for changes in strategy without having to help the client deal with the complex issues of implementation.[3]

STUDIES AND THEIR METHODOLOGY

Studies have three main phases:

- Diagnosis *(Interim Report)*

- Planning (or Remedy) *(Final Report)*

- Action (Concluding Conferences and Review Conference).

In the first phase, Diagnosis, there is a clear agreed identification by the participants in the Study — typically 20 to 40 senior managers — of the real issues facing the organisation. These issues, and their relative importance, vary from company to company. Some issues in over 20 Studies have been:

- An unrealistic mission

- An unclear, opportunistic strategy

- Product- rather than market-driven

- A faulty, unshared strategic process, or none at all

- Inadequate or inaccurate information on which to make decisions

- Historical rather than future-oriented information

- A management style or leadership out of tune with the changing needs of the organisation

- Lack of coherence in the top team

- Confusion about structure and roles

- Changing businesses and unchanging structures — new wine in old bottles

- Centralisation versus decentralisation

- The relationship with headquarters — freedom/ initiative versus necessary control

- Management capability lagging behind the organisation's growth — a need for management and organisation development as an integral part of a comprehensive strategy

- Lack of manpower forecasting or succession planning

- People who do what they're told or who act entrepreneurially

- A self-reinforcing, closed culture — we do only what we know

- Quality taking second place to expediency or the bottom-line — short-termism building up future problems

- Frustration with faulty communication and particularly with the quality of meetings.

The issues identified are rarely surprising. The force of the analysis comes from the force and clarity of the consensus with which the participants express the issues, something which seldom happens in the day-to-day running of the organisation. Issues lie buried under conformity until there is a crisis. They then surface in recrimination.

As well as clarifying the issues, the first phase gives a unifying catharsis and the increase in confidence that comes from facing reality together. Bill Critchley put it thus:

> Although diagnosing the present can be a painful process, it can also generate a great deal of energy and make the need for change starkly apparent, as those involved in the process reveal their dissatisfaction with certain aspects of the organisation for which they work.[4]

An IMI study of the 1970s stressed the possibilities of this new vision:

> We subscribed to what has been called the paradoxical theory of change: that is, that people, groups, organisations and, indeed, entire communities are stimulated to change when confronted with the situation "as it is".[5]

The organisation is freed up.

The second phase of the work, Planning, provides a sharper clarity and a deeper understanding of the issues — not just what happens, but why. The issues are now in priority — of long-term importance rather than of urgency. There is a rich harvest of views about what should be done. The organisation is moving towards remedying what it has itself diagnosed.

The third and final phase, Action, is the climax of the work. The participants have reflected upon a mass of accurate data — they know where they stand. There is now a concern to have done with diagnosis and to move on to action. The issues are out on the table for all to see. In a two-day conference, meticulously planned, the participants come together for the first time and discuss with the chief executive what they believe should be done. The quality of the output of these conferences is high, partly because of the release of motivation, partly because the participants are so well informed. The conferences are recorded: there is an agreed agenda for future action.

The chief executives and participants in recent Studies decided to revisit the Study in a one-day conference six to nine months following its completion. This is now standard practice.

A Study is not a management audit. It has nothing to do with how good an individual participant is at his or her job. We are concerned only with the participant's views of the organisation and the issues it faces.

The methodology is as simple as the basic premises underlying the work.

The essential element is two one-to-one three-hour (or longer) confidential interviews. The first interviews are largely unstructured. From them comes an *Interim Report* (the first Diagnostic phase) setting out the issues. It is circulated in strict confidence to all participants.

The *Interim Report* also gives the results of questionnaires completed by the participants before the interviews and on which they get individual feedback. The questionnaires would cover:

• Age distribution now and in five years' time

• Length of service with the company

• Length of service in present job

• Educational background

- Participation in post-experience training
- Language skills
- An organisation climate survey
- An organisation blockages survey
- A strength of culture survey
- A survey of comparative culture types.

The second interview (the second phase) is more structured and is based on the participant's reading of the *Interim Report*. From this work comes the *Final Report*, which also contains a commentary by myself.

While I take verbatim notes during the interviews, participants' views are incorporated in the *Interim* and *Final Reports* in a way in which they are completely unattributable, thus maintaining total trust and confidentiality, a *sine qua non* for the work.

As noted above, the final phase is a recorded conference where the participants and the chief executive, on the basis of their study of the two *Reports*, agree the priorities and what should now be done. A verbatim report on the conference is circulated to participants. It is the conscience of the Study and is the subject of the review conference.

The "population" for the work must fulfil two conditions: one, it must be of sufficient breadth and depth to give an accurate reading of the organisation; two, it must be politically acceptable — managers must see objective criteria for who is included and, more important, who is not.

The population to attain both objectives is: the chief executive; those who report to him; those who report to them. In other words, selection is by rank or office, not, so far as is possible, arbitrary.

WHAT IS TRUTH?

"What is truth?" asked Pontius Pilate. People see things from different perspectives, but, when there is consensus, as there always is, the work is as near as possible to objective truth, i.e., to people seeing the same thing from different perspectives.[6]

Once more with feeling: efficiency comes from enthusiasm. Enduring enthusiasm can be generated only with participation. A precondition for participation is consensus. Participation is not soft. It means taking account of views that may not coincide with your own, that may not be so well informed as your own — but that must be dealt with simply because they exist. Otherwise they remain as stumbling blocks, many of them unseen.

Studies work only in organisations where there is strong leadership[7] and where the central belief is that people are fundamentally decent and like to work, and that encouragement brings out the best in them. Studies would never work in an organisation where the prevailing view is that people are lazy and irresponsible and need to be driven and watched. The Studies succeed because of the total trust generated, and this can happen only in lively successful organisations. (I am not a company doctor.)

Strategy may be clear to the people at the very top of an organisation but we know that, for every level through which information passes, it can lose up to half its meaning. Weinshall and Kyriasis have worked out the implications of this loss in a simple mathematical model:

> In a five-level hierarchy, with four gaps among the levels, the amount of the innermost truth of the lowest level reaching the upper level of the CEO is one-third (of the "truth") at the power of four (gaps), 1/81, a little more than one per cent. The same is true when the communication flows downwards. Thus in a hierarchy of five levels under the same assumptions, only somewhat more than one per cent of what the CEO really thinks and feels is reaching the first line of managers.[8]

The issue is further confused by the way people manage information.

> One of the commonest reasons for giving information is *telling people what they want to hear*. If the person who is asking for information is somebody whose opinion you value this may become more pronounced, but in any case it is much easier to pass on good news than bad . . . The person seeking information may contribute; *we do not always want the truth* . . . A person may give misleading or unhelpful information because they *do not think the asker needs to know* . . . It is always difficult to stop people *telling you what is supposed to be the case*.[9]

All of this results in more pressure and less time for thought because, from below, there is the constant need for guidance; from above, the constant need for checking. Time is wasted dealing with incidents, most of which are of the organisation's own making: they could well have been avoided if earlier decisions were made with a clear understanding of where the organisation was going and why.

And preoccupation with incident management lessens the organisation's responsiveness. Opportunities can be missed. Without a clear, shared strategy, opportunities may not even be seen: "Opportunity comes to pass, not to pause."[10] In Rabelais' words:

> Opportunity has only a forelock: once it has passed you by, nothing you can do will bring it back, it is bald behind and never again turns its head.

A clear, shared strategy means decisions are taken confidently and freely at all key levels in the organisation. Creativity is released — but within an agreed strategic context. The number of strategic choices is reduced: the greater the choice, the greater the uncertainty. The greater the uncertainty, the more people are unfree.

The true measure of the work is the amount of change it generates. A Study can generate considerable change. However, in some instances, the change can take some time before it seeps right through the organisation. There will have been one or two defining moments on the way, but change works best when people find themselves doing new things in different ways while hardly noticing.

Origin and Development

The above outlines the information all participants get
before a Study begins. It summarises as succinctly as I
can what they may expect. It suffers from the fact that it
is one-sided communication (an oxymoron). It is helped
somewhat by preliminary meetings with the barons —
i.e., those who report directly to the CEO. That at least
gives an opportunity for close questioning and for il-
lustrations (unattributable) from previous Studies.

The origin of the Studies probably came from conversations with Teddy Weinshall, against the background of a conviction, reinforced in my years in the
IMI, that managers learn little from what they are told
and a lot from what they do.[11] The Studies, in their basic format of two series of interviews, have hardly
changed over the years. What goes on inside that format has got better.

I can see more clearly the fundamental problems and
their tentacles and am more open to ambiguity and
paradox. And yet, having said that, being forced by
writing this book to go back and read the first Studies,
they are as accurate in their diagnosis as more recent
ones. The Irish proverb, *tagann ciall le haois* (wisdom
comes with age), may not necessarily apply. What is
true is that with experience there is a deeper well of
knowledge to draw on and, perhaps, better judgement.[12] There is a concomitant danger of jumping too
quickly to conclusions. The only way to avoid that
danger is to listen, to record scrupulously what participants say — never to "adjust" the data — and then to

base conclusions only on those data and to eschew any "notions" developed en route.

There is another safeguard. Notes taken at the first interview are read over to the participants at the second one. They are asked, "Is that what you said?" I have never had a participant who wanted to have notes changed. Finally, the participants have before them all the data on which the summaries/conclusions are based.[13] This is a built-in check on the accuracy of the summaries. The process is transparent: no bias, no hidden agenda, no special pleading, nothing concealed — with one exception: a private report to the chief executive containing only participants' views of him. (See next section.)

(The Strategic Cascade, shown on the following page, is not a questionnaire used in the interviews. It is, however, a useful reminder to give to a participant towards the end of an interview to jog memory, to see if anything has been left out.)

THE CHIEF EXECUTIVE

Inevitably, in the course of an interview, participants will talk spontaneously about the chief executive. This is never invited. To do so would be not only distasteful but would damage the interview which has to be both objective and intimate. For an outsider to ask participants what they think of the boss would be offensive. Momentary catharsis for the participant could be followed by feelings of guilt and disloyalty and injure the critical continuing relationship of trust with the adviser.

The Strategic Cascade

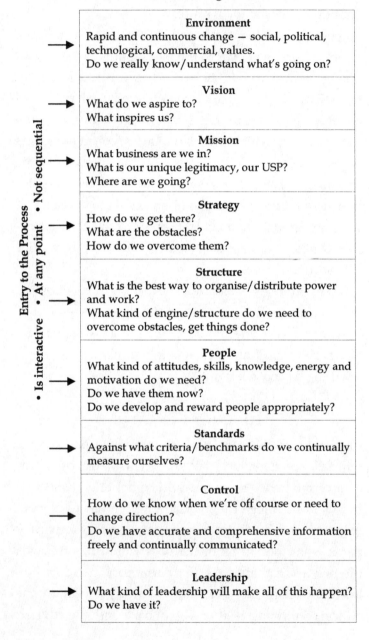

Environment
Rapid and continuous change — social, political, technological, commercial, values.
Do we really know/understand what's going on?

Vision
What do we aspire to?
What inspires us?

Mission
What business are we in?
What is our unique legitimacy, our USP?
Where are we going?

Strategy
How do we get there?
What are the obstacles?
How do we overcome them?

Structure
What is the best way to organise/distribute power and work?
What kind of engine/structure do we need to overcome obstacles, get things done?

People
What kind of attitudes, skills, knowledge, energy and motivation do we need?
Do we have them now?
Do we develop and reward people appropriately?

Standards
Against what criteria/benchmarks do we continually measure ourselves?

Control
How do we know when we're off course or need to change direction?
Do we have accurate and comprehensive information freely and continually communicated?

Leadership
What kind of leadership will make all of this happen?
Do we have it?

Entry to the Process • At any point • Not sequential • Is interactive

Spontaneous remarks are another thing. Participants know that what they say is being written down. They know, because they have been told, that the private report on the chief executive will be unlaundered but made in a form that maintains unattributability.

In one Study, a participant noted that I was writing quickly while he unburdened himself of some fruity opinions of his CEO. He said, "You're not writing that down?"

I said, "I am."

"You're not going to give him all that?"

I said, "I am."

"He'll go berserk."

He did not go berserk. A chief executive who did not want to know what his troops thought of him would not be worth his salt (and would not have commissioned a Study in the first place). A personality change would be too much to hope for as a result of his learning experience, but I have noticed a bit more listening, a bit more appreciation of subordinates, a modification of ballistic behaviour.

What happens following a Study depends absolutely on the chief executive.[14] If he has not really heard and absorbed what the organisation is saying to him, then nothing or not much will happen.

The chief executive is locked into a Study from day one until its completion, but he is not a prisoner of the recommendations of his colleagues. Firstly, only a chief executive who has confidence in his organisation (and his colleagues) will commission a Study. Secondly, his personal authority will not derive from his having to win every argument. Finally, the recommendations are drawn from the deep pool of common sense in all organisations that possess the characteristics for an effective Study. There will, of course, particularly in the first (*Interim*) *Report*, be criticism and maybe some blame-laying and cynicism. These are a necessary part of the catharsis. They disappear as the Study focuses increasingly on what needs to be done. I never met with daft or destructive ideas in a Study.

Notes

1. Stephen Swartz (1989), "The Challenges of Multidisciplinary Consulting to Family-Owned Businesses", *Family Business Review*, Vol. 2, No. 4, Winter, p. 333.

2. Elliott Jacques (1990), "In Praise of Hierarchy", *Harvard Business Review*, January–February, p. 128.

3. Robert O. Metzger (1990), "With So Many Consultants, Why Aren't We Better?" *Journal of Management Consulting*, July, p. 13.

4. Bill Critchley, quoted in: "Visions of the Present", *Strategic Direction*, April 1994, p. 12.

5. Liam Gorman, Ruth Handy, Tony Moynihan and Roderick Murphy (1974), *Managers in Ireland*, Dublin: Irish Management Institute, pp. 177–8.

6. "There was a time when you could assume that an intelligent person looking for the truth was guided by the most basic of scientific intuitions: nature will give you a lift only if you're going her way. The fallaciousness of the *ad hominem* argument and the argument from consequence, for example, was so obvious that the anticipation of the embarrassment you would feel if you invoked such arguments was sufficient to preclude you

doing so. In social science today we can no longer make this assumption. Even if we continue to maintain that we are dealing with intelligent people, we find no way to maintain the belief that such people act on an impulse to find the truth. Instead, we find large and increasing numbers of ideologues who act not as if nature is something to be discovered, no matter what she should turn out to be, but rather as if she is a handmaiden whose purpose is to satisfy one's psychological and ideological needs. Lacking the rudimentary scientific impulse of self-refutation (i.e., if you are happy with the conclusions reached by your research, double-check and triple-check those conclusions), the ideologue assesses truth not by its concordance with reality, but by its concordance with psychological and ideological needs. Whether incompetence or deceitfulness is to blame is neither here nor there; the work itself is effectively both incompetent *and* deceitful. And once the desire for truth is not the only permissible impulse, one is no longer playing the same game we are." Steven Goldberg (1996), "The Erosion of the Social Sciences", *Dumbing Down*, New York: W.W. Norton and Company, pp. 97–8.

7. "Only an organisation with strong leadership will look within itself for causes of problems that can be blamed easily on outside forces." David E. Berlew and Douglas T. Hall (1966), "The Socialisation of Managers: Effects of Expectations on Performance", *Administrative Science Quarterly*, Vol. 11, No. 2, p. 207.

8. Theodore D. Weinshall and Harry C. Kyriasis (1986), "Behavioural Aspects of Outsiders Helping Managements to Improve Their Organisations", paper presented to the International Association of Applied Psychology conference, Jerusalem, July, p. 7.

9. David Sims (1993), "Coping with Misinformation", *Management Decision*, Vol. 31, No. 5, p. 19. See also: Theodore D. Weinshall and Yael-Anna Raveh (1983), *Managing Growing Organisations: A New Approach*, Chichester: John Wiley & Sons.

10. Jefferson Smurfit, quoted by Michael W.J. Smurfit (n.d.), "The International Growth of an Irish Enterprise", The Dillon-Malone Lecture, Dublin: Jefferson Smurfit Group PLC, p. 4.

11. Theodore Weinshall and Harry C. Kyriasis, *op. cit.*, pp. 1–26.
    The Studies were first described in a paper given to the Fellows
    of the International Academy of Management in New York in
    October 1985 and published in the *Irish Marketing Review*, Vol.
    1, Spring 1986, pp. 148–52.

12. "The *investment* cost of intuition is far higher, for one cannot be
    (effectively) intuitive unless one has intimate knowledge of the
    subject in question, which sometimes requires years to develop.
    Good analysis, in contrast, is available anywhere clever ana-
    lysts can get their hands on good hard data." Henry Mintzberg
    (1994), *The Rise and Fall of Strategic Planning*, London: Prentice
    Hall, p. 325.

13. Charles Margerison quotes Chris Argyris approvingly:

    "Chris Argyris is committed to the study of real life manage-
    ment practice and feeding back the information to the partici-
    pants as a basis for helping them improve their own
    performance. He puts forward three conditions which he feels
    consultant advisers should uphold. These are:

    • Valid and useful information has to be generated by the
      consultant and fed back in a discussion form to the client.

    • The options presented to the client should give him a free
      choice, rather than the consultant providing the client with
      a *fait accompli*.

    • Internal commitment means that the consultant should
      work to facilitate understanding and agreement amongst
      participants so they can work positively and effectively."

    Charles Margerison (1988), *Managerial Consulting Skills: A Prac-
    tical Guide*, Aldershot: Gower, p. 85.

14. "Unless both the client and consultant accept responsibility, they
    will be unlikely to create meaningful change." Eileen C. Shapiro,
    Robert G. Eccles and Trina L. Soske (1993), "Consulting: Has the
    Solution Become Part of the Problem?", *Sloan Management Review*,
    Summer, p. 92.

Chapter 3

THE CLIENT: THE CHIEF EXECUTIVE PLUS

If circumstances lead me, I will find
Where truth is hid, though it were hid indeed
Within the centre.

— Hamlet

LEADERSHIP

This is the shape of a Study:

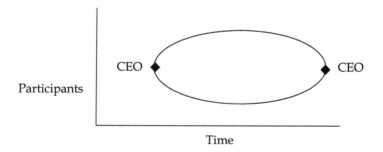

It starts and ends with the chief executive. He is the primary client. He first commissions the Study. He finally decides on the changes to be made in the organisation. However, in the course of the Study, the organisation, the individual participants, become the client. Their views constitute the *Reports*. They make the recommendations. They ultimately carry them out.

My job is to listen, to encourage openness by showing that I understand what participants are saying, gently to question assumptions. My key role is to synthesise: to distil from the mass of facts, opinions, prejudices and convictions the heart of the matter. And this synthesis can happen only inside one head. You are dealing with much soft and some hard data. It is not a question, as Mintzberg pointed out (see endnote 12, Chapter 2), of a clever analyst getting his hands on hard data. It is intuitive knowledge of the process. And it is a matter of trust, of the chemistry between myself and the participants.

It is the chemistry between myself and the chief executive that opens the door to the organisation.

In 1986, I set out to write a book on *Leadership*, by the simple expedient of getting leaders to talk about themselves. I ran into trouble straight away with the title: a number of participants felt uncomfortable with it and Ken Whitaker (*q.v.*) initially refused outright because he "associated the leadership concept with the Führer Prinzip of the dictatorships which clouded so much of our adult experience". I said, "Well, people in leadership positions." This helped. Leaders or not, chief executives are in leadership positions.[1]

Leadership is a job, a function, not a set of characteristics. The criterion for identifying leaders is the influence they wield: leaders are those who influence the activities of other people. Authority of itself does not make people leaders. We shall see below that leaders can be perceived by followers in different ways. Managerial leadership exists only from the moment a subordinate perceives it as leadership. So long as a subordinate has no decisive motive to accept it or to put up with it, very little will happen.

The chief executives in the Studies were strong leaders. Otherwise they would not have commissioned the Studies. However, again as we shall see, the characteristic that most concerned their subordinates was aloofness. Several were seen as operating above and apart from the organisation — like this:

That is a classic image: the remote, heroic figure. (And that is the way many leaders see themselves.[2])

Above is a more subtle, less clear, more ambiguous role. It is the one that may have currency in the future, if only because the future may be more ambiguous than the past. Once it was "Follow me". Now we are a negotiating society. If we are to apply new solutions to new problems, we shall have to part with some received ideas about authority and hierarchy. That does not mean that leaders have to court popularity. That cuts a pathetic figure. And that is not what their followers expect of them. Two things are needed (there are always at least two): a firm hand on the tiller and subordinates who are able to influence the course of events from their knowledge and their responsibilities.

When, on the Pocock Committee,[3] we looked at the educational and training needs of European managers, we noted that the first challenge the manager faced was the prevalence of contradiction. Economic ends must respond to social needs, but, if the economic end is not put first, the social end may be unattainable. Or, again, managerial power diminishes, while managerial responsibilities grow. Thus the tolerance and mastery of ambiguities will be central to the job of leadership. This central point is taken up again in the *Conclusion*.

There will be few set approaches, never mind solutions. A continually searching mind, with skills of analysis, will be more important than any portfolio of acquired knowledge. We did not, in Pocock, throw the baby out with the bath water. We did not say that traditional skills were redundant. There is not much point in discussing the finer points of leadership with a manager who cannot analyse a balance sheet. What we did say was that the new pressures were social, political and economic all at the same time, that managers needed new skills as well as the old ones.

There are many perspectives you can use in looking at leadership. To summarise would merely do violence to reality. Nevertheless, there are four points that are significant. First, the leader, while identifying with the organisation as it is at present, must influence what the organisation is to become. Second, unlike other participants, the leader is responsible for the total enterprise and not for a part of the organisation: leaders must, above all, shun cronyism. Third, leaders are subject to stresses and internal conflicts. They must not project some of their internal strife outwards onto the situation they are coping with. Tony O'Reilly, head of Heinz and of Irish companies, said,

> Sometimes, anger and irritation will show but I have analysed my irritation as a management instrument and found that I am less effective when I

am angry and irritated. I am not as eloquent, not as thoughtful, and I'm often wrong.[4]

Finally, leaders are both insiders and outsiders. They have a dual orientation. They must manage forces both from within the organisation and from outside.

From the subordinate's point of view, what the leader *does* is critical. Leaders need to make clear the purposes of their organisations and the standards of performance that are expected. They need to give feedback on performance, to listen to other views and to be genuinely open to influence. They need to make the decisions that are theirs to make, and not pass the buck.

And successful leaders generate what David Berlew has called "organisational excitement". They see not only what is but also what could be, and they have the ability to inspire others with their vision and strength of purpose.[5]

John Kotter says management is about coping with complexity, particularly in that twentieth century phenomenon, the large organisation.

> Leadership, by contrast, is about coping with change. Part of the reason is that the business world has become more competitive and more volatile.[6]

This is too fine a distinction for me.

Warren Bennis has written: "Books on leadership are often as majestically useless as they are pretentious."[7] (That did not stop him writing about it.) Chester Barnard said, "Leadership has been the subject of an extraordinary amount of dogmatically stated non-sense."[8] Barnard was echoed alliteratively by Micklethwait and Wooldridge:

> Within the wayward word-spattering world of management theory, no subject has produced more waffle than leadership. By one count there are 130 different definitions . . .[9]

Steiner enumerated 14 qualities a CEO needed. Still with mystic numbers, Covey prescribed seven "habits" and Kanter seven "skills and sensibilities".[10]

Bartlett and Ghoshal have written:

> Leaders share a surprisingly consistent philosophy. First, they place less emphasis on following a clear strategic plan than on building a rich, engaging corporate purpose. Next, they focus less on formal structural design and more on effective management processes. Finally they are less concerned with controlling employees' behaviour than with developing their capabilities and broadening their perspectives. In some, they have moved beyond the old doctrine of strategy, structure, and systems to a softer, more organic model built on the development of purpose, process, and people.[11]

In the Irish Management Institute, with Dermot Egan, we collaborated with the Institute of Personality Assessment and Research of the University of California at Berkeley in conducting a psychological study of 37 practising "leaders in Irish management".[12] This is what they thought of *themselves*:

1. Able to arrive at sound common-sense decisions.

2. Able to size up a problem and distinguish between major and minor issues.

3. Good at evaluating plans; able to diagnose strong and weak points in a plan quickly and accurately.

4. Thinks far ahead; plans with long-range objectives in mind.

5. Able to make proper use of subordinates, giving credit to their achievements.

And these were characteristics they felt *least described themselves*:

1. Tends to slight the contribution of others; takes undue credit for himself.

2. Easily discouraged; needs help and encouragement to do his best work.

3. Somewhat given to bluffing; claims to know more than he does.

4. Is relatively uninformed on most subjects other than his speciality.

5. Many of his ideas turn out to be impractical.

This is how they described the *ideal manager*:

1. Thinks far ahead; plans with long-range objectives in mind.

2. Stimulating to other people; seems to catalyse others into more original and productive endeavour than they would otherwise achieve.

3. Good at evaluating plans; able to diagnose strong and weak points in a plan quickly and accurately.

4. Able to size up a problem and distinguish between major and minor issues.

5. Can take other people's ideas and concepts and fashion them into practical programmes for the development of new products and services.

And these were the characteristics they felt *least described the ideal manager*:

1. Finds it difficult to be interested in the work of others and prefers to spend his energies on his own work.

2. Easily discouraged; needs help and encouragement to do his best work.

3. Tends to slight the contribution of others; takes undue credit for himself.

4. Puts business values above all others.

5. Is relatively uninformed on most subjects other than his speciality.

The research concluded: "On the whole, their perception of their real self is rather close to what they think of as the ideal."

As we saw in the previous chapter, my own Studies have as a basis that truth — conformity with fact, agreement with reality — is most likely to be found where a number of people see (and can define) the same thing from different angles, where there is consensus about that which is, not what should or might be.

To explore the question of how CEOs appear to their immediate subordinates, I compare here (for the first time) what the participants in 12 Studies said about their 12 chief executives. There was such high consensus about both the good and the bad characteristics of these men that the participants could almost have been talking about the same person. All that was necessary was to select at random some of the verbatim comments from each of the 12 *Reports* to give a picture of a composite CEO — "John Smith".

The IMI/Berkeley research, and much of the current literature on leadership, gives a top-down view. What follows gives a bottom-up, a follower's, view. It is, however, not only a view of how followers see their leaders; it also reveals followers' needs.

Confucius believed in a loyal opposition. Asked how to serve a prince, he replied: "Tell him the truth even if it offends him".[13] Before a new Pope is enthroned, a friar stands in front of him and lights a piece of hempen rope which flares and goes out. This is to remind the Pope of the vanities of leadership. Mediaeval monarchs employed a court jester who could say in jest what the courtiers could not say in seriousness.

The verbatim comments that follow are presented in the form used throughout the Studies. Views on strategy, structure, etc. — the issues — would be recorded in similar verbatim fashion, then summarised by me.

"JOHN SMITH" SEEN FAVOURABLY

The good John Smith is seen by his subordinates as an inspiring leader, dedicated, likeable, a big loss if he left. He takes the long view. He is accessible and supportive, stays in touch. He lets you get on with it, but looks for results. He has integrity and is decisive. He knows the business but may have to change as it changes.

John Smith is seen as an inspiring leader, dedicated, likeable, a big loss if he left:

"John Smith is a big, big, leader, an enlightened despot, very wise."

"John Smith is a leader. A leader is someone people do things for."

"This company has a soul — due to John Smith."

"One man reigns supreme and he makes all the decisions. There is a respect for his decisions and they are accepted."

"The policy led by John Smith can be very strong. When he tells us what to do, there is reflection behind it and he insists that it be done. That is very positive. It's good to feel that the big boss is someone we can believe in and rely on. He's a leader."

"John Smith's faults are far outweighed by his ability get people to lift their game."

"John Smith has undoubtedly been good for us. He has opened up areas by his leadership as distinct from his management."

"When John Smith takes something on he throws himself into it."

"This company is a monument to John Smith."

"John Smith's faith in the company was like an electrical charge."

"John Smith is totally dedicated to this company. Is it really worth it? For his health? He has a hunger to expand at a hell of a rate. One of the drawbacks is that he may expect too much from people."

"John Smith is a workaholic and a supreme technician."

"You are likely to find John Smith in the office on a Saturday evening — he lives for his work."

"John Smith saw the hard times. He is a great, great guy. I enjoy his company immensely."

"My first impression of John Smith was that he was very friendly with a great sense of humour. He is quiet and even-tempered. He knew his business and knew what he didn't know."

"I have learned a lot from John Smith. I admire his style, his shrewdness."

"It would be a disaster for the company if John Smith left."

"We have a small team. There are gaps in it. There will be a great culture shock when John Smith goes. He has given the company his whole life."

He takes the long view:

"Our success is due to John Smith's breadth of vision."

"John Smith is very good at asking why."

"I'd like to have met John Smith in my mid-20s. He has great foresight. Sometimes he can go too far ahead. Sometimes he sees a business where maybe there won't be one — maybe in ten years' time."

"I have the utmost respect for John Smith. He has tremendous vision. He excels when he's distanced from something. He remains far too emotional about what he's doing in the business."

"Without John Smith's vision and foresight, we could never have changed. I would never have said that the changes he has succeeded in were possible."

"I have the height of respect for John Smith. If he was not here I would not be talking to you today, but I have to say that his interests lie not in maintenance management but in the sexy things."

"When John Smith visits a factory, he always finds something and always has good ideas. He has a global perspective."

"John Smith is truly a universal man."

He is accessible and supportive, stays in touch:

"When John speaks about my problems, he recognises me. When he understands my problem, I'm highly motivated."

"I saw John Smith talk to a blue collar worker and you could not tell the difference between them. It was terrific."

"John Smith appreciates very much if you tell him what you really think."

"In fairness, John Smith does get involved in helping you take the hill."

"There are many live issues in the organisation that John Smith brought to the fore."

"The most significant thing was the way John Smith went around to every single member of staff and shook their hands. I have never heard a single word against him."

"John Smith is tremendously loyal to his people. At times I find this frustrating. He is very bad at sacking people. He'll find a place for them where they're better off. He is also a powerful disciplinarian on himself. He has learned to organise himself — as he has had to in this business."

"I have no problem knocking on John Smith's door. He is a very tough man. He would give you a bollocking, but it would be good for the business. He would keep you on your toes."

"John Smith is a very hands-on guy. He likes to know what everybody is doing — we probably all work like that. John Smith is constantly in touch."

"I can honestly say I love John Smith. I enjoy his company, even when he digs his heels in."

"I have got great support from John Smith. A clap on the back from him means a hell of a lot to me."

"It's very important that John Smith is the continuing charismatic head of the organisation — particularly with people down the line. He has a very good way with staff. OK — he can't be involved with the day-to-day stuff and anyway he gets bored and irritated with it. But he can't lose touch with the troops."

"John Smith has tremendous balls in going for things. He may not understand the area he's going into but he picks it up on the way. He can be very radical in his approach. He will listen to anybody — it can do no harm. That's why we've no corporate policy."

"In particular circumstances last year the consideration I got from the company was unbelievable. John Smith was very caring and understanding, full of thought and kindness. Unbelievably good."

"John Smith's decisions do not always prevail. He is much less impatient or aggressive now than he was several years ago."

"John Smith is a good manager. He will try to manipulate a conversation so that you think his idea is yours."

"People like to work with John Smith. He is not seen as a shark. In some ways, he should be seen as a softie — but he's not. He's a great listener, but he would not change from what he wanted to do!"

"John Smith has no inhibitions and lets his hair down completely at staff parties."

He lets you get on with it, but looks for results:

"John Smith is anti imposing anything on anybody."

"John Smith is able to delegate. I have seen him let people get on with it. But he will do it very selectively. He treats different people in different ways."

"John Smith gives people plenty of scope to be their own person."

"People are very happy about John Smith because they know him for a very long time. John Smith's style is certainly not one of constant checking nor does he cross lines to subordinate managers."

"John Smith sees his job as to put pressure but everybody knows it's a game. He gets away with it because he's a good guy who knows the business and he knows also how to use the kind word."

"I feel considerable stress passed on from John Smith. Sometimes it upsets me but it's up to yourself to manage the stress. And then, without that level of stress, would we have the lively organisation we have now?"

He has integrity and is decisive:

"John Smith overflows with integrity and it comes across. He is a marathon man rather than a miler. He's in for the long haul."

"John Smith has never let me down. He's the ultimate in integrity. He is an almighty asset to the company and he is totally under-utilised. He has an incredibly good style. His ability to communicate to outsiders is terrific."

"When you meet John Smith, he does not put you under pressure, but gets his way with you. It's always a very personal way, full of integrity."

"John Smith is the ultimate in integrity. He'll never let you down — but he always wants to keep his options open."

"One of John Smith's strengths is that he is such a nice guy. He is not a bastard at all — at least from my perspective. He's very principled."

"John Smith is a terrific decision-taker."

"John Smith has superb balls about taking a decision."

"The Study is about consensus, but sometimes tough decisions are needed and then you need one man to take them — a lonely position."

He knows the business but may have to change:

"When I met John Smith, he had spent an hour or two in my factory. In that short time, he fully understood our problems. He knows his business. He asks the right questions."

"When John Smith says something, everybody comes to attention. The point is he is the one who knows the business best. I don't get the same response from anyone else."

"John Smith's role has to change now from what it was."

"Nobody could have done what John Smith did but now it has to be different."

"Nobody else could have done what John Smith did. He had a tremendous charisma. He will now have to change — but so will the people beneath him."

"JOHN SMITH" SEEN UNFAVOURABLY

The bad Mr Smith is dominant and autocratic. He tends to decide everything. He is remote, aloof, does not tell people what's going on. He, in turn, is not told the truth. His style encourages sycophancy and dependency. He encourages cronyism. He can be inconsistent, moody and emotional. He shows little appreciation.

John Smith is dominant and autocratic:

"This company is absolutely a one-man-show. We have in John Smith a kind of genius, but a one-man-show is frustrating for other people. I have never seen an organisation — and I have worked in several — where the top guy can put pressure so deep down into the organisation. I have seen, of course, organisations where the top man is frustrated at the fact that he cannot exert pressure."

"John Smith's dominance can have its downside. The more he asks for participation, the less he'll get it."

"John Smith is heavily dominant, but the chief executive has to set the tone and make the decisions. I would worry about the people who could follow in his footsteps. There is no one with his overall grasp. You can't compare John Smith with anyone else. He has a tremendous air of authority which he can apply in very different circumstances."

"People worry about which way he is thinking. They are trying to say yes to him but at times do not understand what they are saying yes to."

"It's very easy for John Smith to impose his will on some people. He goes ahead when even his immediate allies disagree. Other people will give an appearance of agreement."

"John Smith is a hard task-master, as hard as one would meet."

"John Smith does not like his authority threatened. After a painful incident, I would now be very cautious dealing with him. If he asks for something on one page and gets it on two, he is very sarcastic."

"While John Smith will say we have open systems, he will savage anyone who disagrees with him."

"It's a one-man company dictated by John Smith. I don't know what it is about him, but I freeze in front of him. He has a certain presence that is very off-putting. He's very nice and all that. In terms of communication, it doesn't help. It also affects others. If the phone rings and John Smith wants you, you drop everything and go. From the business side, maybe that is the way to run things. But it makes the organisation seem less human."

"John Smith is a time-bandit. He turned up when I didn't expect him. You can find yourself caught off guard. You can't talk back to him about this. He steals your time arbitrarily. I don't know whether he's aware of it or is aware of it and doesn't care."

"John Smith has the ability to kill the incentive. He is the best in the world to tell them to go ahead and run it, sign the cheques — but he still likes to go in and interfere. He gives power and then takes it back. Some people will say that it would be better if he was not here all the time. People feel they are watched. But then if you got good people you wouldn't have that concern."

"John Smith will attempt to steam-roll you and if you do confront him he will use his position even more. He'll say he doesn't want to run the business, but he loves hands-on."

"John Smith would walk all over you if you let him."

"People tremble at John Smith."

"John Smith has got very fatherly in his approach. He has developed a paternalistic type of concern."

He tends to decide everything:

"John Smith wants every decision to be made by himself. He holds the cards to his chest. He should delegate a lot more. To an extent, he manages by fear."

"John Smith's real skill is in dealing with top people — the great man who built the company. He should not get involved in hands-on management. He has a tremendous presence in dealing at senior level. But the hands-on is causing some problems. He would find it extremely difficult to let go. He has a tendency to do the jobs for the people he has hired to do those jobs. And, if he is doing their jobs, he is not doing the strategic job."

"John Smith tries to keep too close to so many things. He should know what's happening but there are other people to do it. There are channels to keep him informed."

"Everybody has a need to see and touch John Smith but not in managing their operations, where he's wasting his time, concerning himself with detail."

"John Smith wants to be the final decision-maker in everything. People won't grow unless they're trusted. We all need clout to succeed. I could not run a business that I could not win the respect for. John Smith does not make people accountable enough and make them responsible."

"The people in the organisation who do the strategy are John Smith and John Smith and John Smith."

"It is an extremely autocratic organisation. There is no consensus management. John Smith makes the decisions with a couple of people close to him putting a few words in his ear. He can't do it any longer. He now needs well-informed experts around him. However, I can't imagine the organisation without him. While he's around, it will be an autocratic organisation."

"John Smith will always solve the problem. He likes to pretend to know everything about everything."

"With John Smith if you asked a question and got an answer you were stuck with it."

"The reason John does not release his authority is that we do not have a clear, shared strategy. If he had that, he could release that authority. I don't, in fact, think a strategy exists."

"No matter what the Study says, there will be no change until John Smith decides."

He is remote, aloof, does not tell people what's going on:

"He could at least walk down the corridor."

"John Smith does not open up to anybody. He has the benefit of a very strong and loyal team. If only he would tell you what's going on. If John shared his problems, the team would be unbeatable."

"I will not speak my mind to the boss. I will be guarded. I will not hotly dispute. I will be diplomatic."

"John Smith is very protective of himself. He locks himself away and does not let people know what he is thinking."

"John Smith's loneliness is a lot of his own making."

"I would move heaven and earth for John Smith, but I would like to know him better, I would like to have his confidence."

"John Smith was a different man five years ago. Why do people withdraw into the fortress? If he only realised that a problem shared is a problem halved. He has a very loyal staff — if only he'd open up. He is still trying to have a hands-on style. He keeps tabs on every aspect of the business."

"John Smith creates an aura of aloofness. Just for him to walk around a plant — MBWA — would do a lot of good. In the old days, he knew the names of the people working on the lines. Not now."

"John Smith gives the impression that you are involved but what he is really thinking is, 'Don't confuse me. My mind's made up.'"

"We're all behind John Smith but we can't tell him what he's done wrong. He has a defensive aura around him."

"I have not seen John Smith for ages. There is no informal walk-in, walk-out. I can't get past his secretary. It is very unsatisfactory."

"Why is this Study being done? Because the CEO is wondering why there is a difference between the

commitment he is expecting and what he is getting. You must take account of his personality. He
became a legend — a tough-talking autocratic CEO
who would give short shrift to people. He's a
strong character who can overpower people. People don't have enough space to be fully themselves. There is always a political relationship with
John Smith. Until we unblock the cork at the top of
the bottle, this Study will not work."

"The only acceptable view is the one John Smith
wants to hear. You're not 'on board' if you don't
agree and you'd be made to feel that and, after
three or four times, you shut up."

"John Smith is the generator of ideas — with the
result that everybody else is reactive. People don't
come to him and say, 'We should do this.'"

"John Smith is quick to jump to conclusions about
people. He is often right but frequently wrong.
He'll be more wrong the more he gets away from
people."

"John Smith has a very good knowledge of the
quality of the people. He is not one bit naïve. But
he is getting increasingly divorced from the nuts
and bolts of the organisation — and this is right —
but it has to be organised for and we are not doing
that."

"I don't know John Smith at all."

He, in turn, is not told the truth:

> "When there is an environment of fear and lack of trust, no one is going to point out that the Emperor has no clothes."

> "John Smith has a very different view of the organisation from the rest of us. That's a message for John Smith rather than the rest of us."

> "John Smith is phenomenal. His vision is fantastic. But no one dares question him. That's dangerous. There is no dialogue."

> "People need to be respected. It's not necessary to humiliate them. The first responsibility of a manager is to know that. When one man with a heavy personality has all the power, he does not listen to advice."

> "Most people have not had an opportunity to say things straight to John Smith."

> "My experience is that consultants go back to John Smith to tell him what he wants."

> "John Smith may have difficulty hearing things he doesn't want to hear."

> "John Smith does not take kindly to criticism — even when it's constructive. If you criticised him you'd find yourself in the deepest drain with the smallest shovel."

> "John Smith says that management don't tell him the truth. But he doesn't listen. He says he wants open communications. The first person who disagrees with something he holds dear is cut down — even publicly. He is exposed as being negative."

"People don't tell each other the truth. That comes from the top."

"It took a lot of effort to talk to you as I did — I have a tremendous loyalty to the company. I worked very hard for it. John Smith does not want to hear unpalatable truths. The majority of people at top management level will not tell him the truth because he doesn't want to hear it. He says he wants to know but his actions indicate otherwise. People are trying to get around things rather than saying them out. This is a cause for concern."

"The biggest problem John Smith has to resolve is where he does not totally trust his team's commitment to his values. And the story that John Smith gets is filtered. They tell him what he likes to hear."

"People fear John Smith. Level after level this is reinforced. This leads to a management style that's not completely wanted by him. When I work with someone who reports directly to him, their main concern is not to lose face with him. When I work with my boss, I can level with him — as I can with the shopfloor workers. If John Smith rules by fear, he will not be told the truth. Of course, it comes back to the strength of an individual's character. It's very important that John Smith knows the 'truth' as defined in the Study, i.e., the consensus among the team, people seeing the same problems from completely different angles. Is John Smith's power monolithic or is it collegial? I think he decides alone."

"John Smith's sources of information are polluted by dependency, by sycophancy. He is totally dependent on the information flows in the organisation and there is too much confidence in the truth-ful transmission of information, a confidence that is misplaced."

"John Smith is a brave man to get Ivor Kenny in to do this Study — he may get a lot more than he bargained for."

His style encourages sycophancy and dependency:

"John Smith has too many people around him who are afraid of their lives of him."

"John Smith wants innovation but he tends to jump at people if they come up with a belief other than his. He can then be deceived into believing that people agree with him."

"The organisation is conformist. While John Smith might want to empower people he might want to give them power only to agree with him."

"The loyalty to John Smith is there but it's condi-tional — it's not blind loyalty."

"What has to be done? John Smith has to get away from being seen as the guy who does all the moti-vating. This causes dependency on him."

"People like to stay on the bright side of the gen-eral, not on the shady side — that's where the greatest growl is going to come from."

"John Smith is a law unto himself. Why should you bother thinking when it is done for you?"

"Compatibility is almost submissiveness. John Smith can't have it both ways. He wants submissiveness and creativity. He goes mad if things are not done his way. He does not like situations over which he does not have control."

"John Smith should accept strong people around him, i.e., people with power. If they don't perform — out. But they should have genuine autonomy."

"There are people who get away with murder because they feed John Smith's ego."

"Perhaps strong leaders throughout the organisation are not sought because you will then have permanent conflict with John Smith."

He encourages cronyism:

"The problem is not John Smith. It's the inner cabinet. People say John Smith is hard, but I have seen the wool being pulled over his eyes. You feel badly after something like that. The people around John Smith are so insecure that they will give the easiest answer all the time."

"John Smith is the boss. He rules with an iron fist but is surrounded by yes-men who reinforce this. He has isolated himself from the world."

"John Smith is the real entrepreneur but he has surrounded himself with people who are afraid of entrepreneurs. He has brought up with himself people who are his direct antithesis. The result is that the entrepreneurial spirit has been killed off."

"The standard of management has been depressed because John Smith likes yes-men around him. I suppose that's natural."

"John Smith is very good at receiving criticism — but it depends on who it is from."

"John Smith is quite good on the political side when he puts his mind to it. He is not a details man. He can be soft on some people and too hard on others."

"John Smith likes nice people and promotes them beyond their competence."

"John Smith is totally protected from the hard realities."

"The management functions below the chief executive are not all angelic — there are strengths and weaknesses and accountability for poor results. But the only person who can resolve those is John Smith. But he has a complex political network where he knows that there are people who support him and some who don't. So he builds alliances."

"The key drivers — the top management — in the company are uncertain."

"John Smith has favourite sons. He likes guys who will bend with him, go with him. He likes guys who'll do what they're told. But he does not like to sit down with guys where things have gone wrong and sort them out or even fire them. He leaves that to others."

"I don't think John Smith is the problem. I would be surprised if he had not shared the strategy with the senior people who, presumably, have signed on. It's the rest of us that things are not shared with. Do the top people feel we don't need to know, that we should concentrate on our own business unit strategy?"

"Conversations take place only in an inner circle. If attempts are not made to involve the senior people, we'll begin to make mistakes. We have senior people who are quite capable of leaving. However, the level of trust is awesome. And nobody has the balls to stand up to John Smith in anything."

"There are only four or five people who have John Smith's ear. A distorted message can get to him so fast, it's extremely dangerous. Indirect bombs are easily thrown, instead of confronting problems or individuals openly. Good people can leave very fast."

He can be inconsistent, moody and emotional:

"Decision-making can, at times, be unpredictable. John Smith may be taking decisions without taking account of the technical information."

"He need not necessarily be always rational. He can blow up and act impetuously."

"John Smith is very conscious of his status and his role. He wants to be seen in a good light by all parts of the organisation. That results in lack of clarity."

"John Smith is autocratic. It's recognised and accepted that he's the leader but what people expect from a leader is consistency right across the company, that his judgements are against the same criteria across the company. I'm afraid that's not the case. If you want to tighten the rope, you have to be consistent and absolutely fair: the fairness must be in the details of your relationship with the business and the people. Words should be carefully chosen so that people are not injured. This is where the autocratic style has its limits. John's behaviour should be more controlled, studied and perhaps a bit softened to be more appropriate to a corporate communication. The company needs to find the right balance between personality and participation. John would need to be clearer about what image he wants to pass on. Image needs control."

"John Smith blows hot and cold, talks off the top of his head."

"John Smith goes through waves of change. There's a struggle going on within him. You get a sense of shifting. We'll have to get the company coherent about this."

"I find it extremely difficult to read John Smith in terms of his motives. He is a victim of his own (perceived) success. He tends to see that everything that happened was due to him. He has come to believe his own propaganda. If you pay people to promote you as successful, your feet come a little off the ground."

"John Smith on a one-to-one in good form is a very nice guy. But his heart rules his actions at times. His emotions guide him. He is terrible at judging people. It's hard to see new people coming in that you would not employ at a junior level."

"John Smith made a major mistake with someone, then, when he realised it, he was very nasty. He lets his emotions guide his actions. He has intense relationships with some and this clouds his judgement. He is too involved. He does not take advice."

"John Smith is like Jekyll and Hyde, he's irrational, changeable. He is very extreme: one minute he is all over you, the next treating you badly. He needs a more balanced, professional approach."

"John Smith is God masquerading as John the Baptist. He alters roles depending on what situation he's in."

"John Smith can be moody. He'd drive you insane when he gets into the nitty-gritty. But he can be tremendously supportive if you're in difficulties."

"If I have a meeting with John Smith, there is no briefing beforehand. I have no idea what way he's going to react. I don't even know whether or not he knows. It might depend on his humour that day."

"John Smith has to adopt chameleon-like behaviour because of all the different pressures."

"John Smith is long-term oriented. He has a fantastic vision of the long term but he's too much stressed by short-term results. That's why there's a contradiction in him."

He shows little appreciation:

"John Smith gives very little support or thanks. He does not seem to be aware of this. It does not increase one's confidence."

"John Smith criticises all the time. He never says, 'Well done.' He should be there in a positive light and should give guidance. He should redefine his role."

"When John Smith says something to you, it's like God talking to you. You take it very personally."

"John Smith has a terribly hurtful way of going on and he's completely unaware of it. There are times when you'd wonder if you should be working in the company at all. And he often forgets your past achievements. He's focused on where he's going often regardless of other people's feelings. He can leave a trail of destruction behind him with people. People have been about to resign and he would not see it."

"John Smith hijacks meetings, tears into people and pillories them."

"John Smith has the habit of occasionally blasting people out of the water at a meeting. I got it — I simply made a factual statement but they were facts he did not want to hear."

"John Smith has a terrible habit of dressing down people in front of others. It's something he should not do."

"John Smith is a terrible man to point out the problems that exist but he is not good at helping you sort them out. It's very easy to complain to a guy. On the other hand, John Smith can get physically involved in the business, involved in detail, in trivia. This can lead to an eye-off-the-ball. I'm not saying he should not be concerned with detail, but he should not be all the time kicking ass. We have become a little bit inhuman. We were always inhuman — we've become more so!"

"John Smith has attempted to galvanise the organisation and has upset a lot of people. He has missed out on the sensitivities of people."

"John Smith would not think of the trauma caused by another person's promotion over somebody's head. People are not seen as individuals."

"John Smith does respect the people he leads but he has difficulty in showing it. He listens to some more carefully than to others. He is autocratic. He has no human feelings. It is all take and no give."

"John Smith does not say thanks."

The views above are a picture of perceived individual behaviour. They also describe a relationship. That relationship is like an electric cable. It contains a warm positive wire and a cold negative one. Which is in the ascendant can depend on circumstances: the smile of appreciation, the frown of humiliation — he is a bad bastard, or, he's not such a bad bastard after all. The good Mr Smith and the bad Mr Smith do not necessarily cancel out one another. In their duality, they represent the human condition.

For all their faults — and their virtues — they ran successful organisations. To suggest that their organisations could have been more successful if they were to behave "better" would be to advance the argument into a theoretical swamp.

From my own observation, danger can come when leaders are seen to have passed their product life-cycle, when they continue to apply to new situations old remedies. The best know this and depart.

Notes

1. Ivor Kenny (1987), *In Good Company*, Dublin: Gill and Macmillan, p. 3. See also *Introduction* to this book.

2. See: Ivor Kenny (1987), *In Good Company*, Dublin: Gill and Macmillan, *passim*.

3. C.C. Pocock (chairman) (1977), *Report of the Committee on Educational and Training Needs of European Managers*, Brussels: European Foundation for Management Development.

4. Tony O'Reilly, quoted in: Ivor Kenny (1987), *In Good Company*, Dublin: Gill and Macmillan, p. 164.

5. "One problem for heads of complex organisations is that they must represent and articulate the hopes and goals of many groups, the young and the old, the unskilled and the professional, the employee and the stockholder, the minority and the majority, union and management. Only the exceptional leader can instinctively identify and articulate the common vision

relevant to such diverse groups. But to fail to provide some kind of vision of the future, particularly for employees who demand meaning and excitement in their work, is to make the fatal assumption that man can and will live by bread alone." David Berlew (1974), "Organisational Excitement", *California Management Review*, Winter, pp. 21–30.

6.   John P. Kotter (1990), "What Leaders Really Do", *Harvard Business Review*, May–June, p. 104.

7.   Warren Bennis and Burt Nanus (1995), *Leaders*, New York: Harper & Row, p. 20.

8.   Quoted in: Thomas R. Horton (1986), *What Works for Me*, New York: Random House, p. 3.

9.   John Micklethwait and Adrian Wooldridge (1997), *The Witch Doctors*, London: Heinemann, pp. 188–9. See also: G.M. Bass (1981), *Stogdills Handbook of Leadership*, New York: Free Press, p. 7: There are almost as many definitions of leadership as there are persons who have attempted to define the concept.

10.   George A. Steiner (1983), *The New CEO*, London: Collier Macmillan Publishers, pp. 48–66; Stephen R. Covey (1992), *The Seven Habits of Highly Effective People: Powerful Lessons in Personal Change*, London: Simon & Schuster, *passim*; Rosabeth Moss Kanter (1989), *When Giants Learn to Dance: Mastering the Challenges of Strategy, Management and Careers in the 1990s*, London: Simon & Schuster, pp. 361–4.

11.   Christopher A. Bartlett and Sumantra Ghoshal (1994), "Beyond Strategy to Purpose", *Harvard Business Review*, November–December, p. 80.

12.   Frank Barron and Dermot Egan (n.d.), *Leaders and Innovators in Irish Management*, Dublin: The Human Sciences Committee of the Irish National Productivity Committee.

13.   Simon Leys (1997), *The Analects of Confucius*, New York: W.W. Norton, p. 34.

THE STUDIES

What follows are seven examples of Studies carried out between 1985 and 1998. There were 12 studies of this type in that period, with about 480 participants and not less than 3,000 hours of interviews. Reports to the participants would typically run to 150/200 pages Interim, *the same for the* Final Report, *with a conference report of about 50 pages — say, 375 pages in all for each Study.*

(Note: my commentaries are taken verbatim from the Reports, *with, in brackets, the date they were written. At the end of each Study there is a short* present (1998) *commentary. Insertions of quotations from other authors are in the main of present date.)*

The seven examples — four private sector and three State companies — were chosen simply by having to leave out the other five. The latter were of such a specific nature that it would be impossible to summarise them here without breaking confidentiality. Brief, non-specific summaries of the five are given in Chapter 11. The spread of principal issues is given in the following table.

	Strategy/ Strategic Process	Capability	Structure	Culture and Style
Study 1	✓✓✓	✓✓		✓
Study 2	✓✓✓		✓✓	
Study 3	✓✓✓✓	✓	✓✓	✓✓✓
Study 4	✓	✓✓		✓✓✓
Study 5	✓✓	✓		
Study 6	✓✓✓	✓	✓✓	
Study 7	✓✓✓	✓	✓✓	

There were four principal issues. Strategy/Strategic Process *was far and away the dominant issue for all Studies (and for the five Studies summarised in Chapter 11) with the exception of Study 4. Markings ✓ (4 highest, 1 lowest) denote the priority each organisation gave to a particular issue. There was no distinction in the ordering of priorities between State and private sector companies.*

Chapter 4

STUDY 1 (1985):
STRATEGY AND THE CEO

INTRODUCTION

Study 1 (1985) was the first of the 12. It was of an Irish company in both the commodity and branded business. The way it began appeared casual or fortuitous, a pattern that was to be repeated through the years. I had never advertised what I was doing. I met the chief executive at the IMI conference in Killarney. He said, "You've left the IMI. Let's talk."

Some weeks later I was on a stage addressing his senior management in the middle of one of their annual away-days. Amid the serious items on their programmes was:

4.00 p.m. Talk. Ivor Kenny.

The conference was concentrated. I'm sure they looked forward to an hour they could doze. The chief executive's introduction was characteristic. "This is Ivor Kenny. I'm sure you know him. He'll be working with us for the next six months."

I had their attention.

When I finished, I invited questions. The first was, "What do you know about our business?" I answered, "Nothing, but I hope you're going to tell me."

The Study stemmed from the chief executive's abiding concern that his company's management capability was not sufficient to attain its objectives quickly enough. There were 31 participants: all the senior management and the CEO.

The Study developed its own objectives as it progressed:

- To give the company more self-knowledge and understanding

- Thereby increasing its self-confidence

- And making it more open to the world about it

- Thus contributing to the quality of its decisions, and

- Accelerating the development of its managers.

The company was going through a profound change — from a relatively simple organisation to a complex one: complex in the number of people working in it, complex in its technologies and products and complex in its international markets.

It would have been unique if its management systems and style were ahead of this growing complexity. In every organisation, the social or management system always lags behind the complexity brought on by growth, technology or new markets.

The ultimate purpose of the Study, then, and the one on which it must finally be judged, was whether or not it helped reduce that gap. It seems to have done so, because I was asked back three years later (see Study 4).

DIAGNOSIS: SUMMARY OF PARTICIPANTS' VIEWS IN THE *INTERIM (DIAGNOSTIC) REPORT*

Strategy is an issue insofar as strategy is perceived not to exist or to be uncertain or unclear. It is the key issue, in that all other issues hang from it/are sub-sets of it.

It must be seen against the background that the company has a skilful and dominant chief executive, who, despite some criticism, is held in high respect.

The main views come out clearly:

- Many people believe there is no overall strategy: at worst that it is made up as we go along; at best that it is only inside the chief executive's head.

- Even those who perceive a strategy perceive it very unclearly, thus creating pressure/dependency on the centre, and some insecurity.

- The unique difficulties of the company, the anxious preoccupation with profitability, push out long-term thinking. "That may be important, but this is urgent." This is helped by the organisation culture, which enjoys crises, but is also becoming a little weary of them.

- There is a strong, perceived need for overall strategy to be a regular, team effort — not the sole prerogative of the chief executive or, worse, of corporate planners, who carry little weight either with the organisation or with themselves.

REMEDY: ADVISER'S COMMENTARY (1985) BASED ON PARTICIPANTS' VIEWS IN THE *PLANNING (SECOND) REPORT*

The most significant view expressed by the participants in the Study was that there was no overall strategy.

The first thing to be done, then, is to get agreement on what we mean by strategy. There is a quite sophisticated view of it in the organisation but, if people were asked to write down their views, they would probably come up with different definitions.

Strategy is, in fact, an elusive and abstract concept. To put it simply: *objectives are the ends* the company seeks to attain, while the *strategy is the means to those ends.* The elusiveness comes from ends and means often shading into one another.

The company has been good at defining, and re-defining, its objectives.

The weakness lies in the fact that there has been no coherent, consistent, comprehensive, continuing strategic planning process, directly involving those managers who carry responsibility for the achievement of corporate objectives. In other words, there is a perceived gap between the company's objectives and the means to attain them.

There have been papers addressing particular issues: e.g., the *Report on Options for Raising Share Capital* (September 1984), the *Research and Development Plan* (January 1984), the *Draft Management Development Programme* (March 1981). These papers do set out strategies.

But the *Five-Year Plan, 27 December 1984*, presumably owing something to the Kami manual, is not really a strategy and, to an outsider, seems to have a high degree of extrapolation from where we are now.[1] More seriously, several of the participants in this Study, who had made contributions to the plan, had never seen it. Critically, the chief executive did not take the lead in the process through which it was prepared. The exercise then, imperfect as it was to begin with, had also, in the way it was subsequently used, minimal significance for Drucker's "futurity of present decisions".

In discussions during the second interviews, the reasons for this were agreed as follows:

- The chief executive was not committed to a *strategic planning process*. What process there was consisted of the away meetings, which seemed to be used mainly to set *general business parameters* and to generate motivation, together with the Executive meetings, where thoughtful discussions on strategy were crowded out by immediate problems.

- The organisation, below the level of the chief executive and his immediate colleagues, was not perceived to be serious about strategic planning. Managers at divisional level, having been told to get on with it, were immersed in day-to-day problems. They felt rewarded for meeting or exceeding budgets, not for formulating elegant long-term plans.

- Thirdly, the organisation lacked strategic competence. Strategic planning is a skill like any other management skill. It has to be *learned*, primarily by doing it, but against some agreed conceptual framework.

All of this is wholly remediable.

In interviews with the chief executive, there was a very clear view of where the organisation was going over the next three to five years, and of the *inter-relatedness* of the decisions necessary to get there. In subsequent interviews with the CEO's immediate colleagues, this clarity was closely shared, if from different perspectives and with differing degrees of enthusiasm.

All that needs to be done to share more widely that clarity, and to add to it, is to establish a continuing process through which those who have to implement strategy can contribute, on an organisation-wide basis, to its formulation.

The benefits to be got from a new process are as follows.

First, instead of "standing back" from the organisation (which, in any event, has negative connotations and is not really wanted by senior management), the chief executive would intervene even more deeply in the organisation, but at a level different, higher and more appropriate than the operational interventions which are now impeding his proper role. He would lead the strategic process.

Second, the genuine participation in the process of senior management could have two significant effects:

1. It would enhance the *quality* (objectivity) of strategic decisions, which would now be based on greater shared knowledge and experience;

2. It would greatly increase the *motivation* of senior managers, who now would be clear where they were going, why they were going there and what support they could get from the organisation as a whole. They would have a greater understanding of the interconnectedness of decisions organisation-wide, leading to greater predictability in their jobs, a better grip on the future. There would be a growth in trust and creativity.

Third, it would be essential for the success of the process that senior management be protected (by the chief executive) from the "that-may-be-important-but-this-is-urgent" syndrome. This would free up the managers beneath them and accelerate the *management development* that the organisation perceives as badly needed, particularly for middle management.

Fourth, senior management will have to take steps to *learn strategic planning*. That is developmental in itself. (The best form of management development is to do something that is both new and relevant.)

Finally, and negatively, if there were to be *no change* in present processes — change which is designed essentially to cope with increasing complexity — if the changing organisation continued to be managed in an unchanging way, there might be some tendency for the organisation to fly apart, putting increasing pressure on the centre to hold it together.

Plans are important. Planning is critical.

ADVISER'S PRESENT (1998) COMMENTARY

Although there was no formal strategy in the company, it was clear from the Study that the CEO and the senior management had a clear vision of where the company was going and how the various parts needed to interact to enable it to get there. The importance of this has been stressed by Mintzberg, who notes that:

> Strategy is not just a notion of how to deal with an enemy or a set of competitors or a market, as it is treated in so much of the literature and in its popular usage. It also draws us into some of the most fundamental issues about organisations as instruments for collective perception and action.[2]

F.A. Maljers expands the point, stressing the inter-relation of all parts of the business in developing the strategy:

> If a global company is to function successfully, strategies at different levels of the business need to inter-relate. The strategy at corporate level must build upon the strategies at lower levels in the hi-erarchy (the bottom-up element of strategy). How-ever, at the same time all parts of the business have to work to accommodate the over-riding corporate goals (the top-down approach). The requirement is to find the right equilibrium. Excessive instruction from the top stifles management creativity. At the same time there must be sufficient direction to al-

low for the interests of all the corporation's stakeholders. In searching for the desired equilibrium it should be remembered that compromise may not lead to the best solution, particularly if it requires combining the worst aspects of different approaches.[3]

One recommendation that emerged from this Study (which I would now express much less prescriptively) related to the importance of positioning the chief executive correctly in the strategic process. Clearly if there was to be time spent on this process, it would have to be at the expense of other involvements, notably operational matters. And yet, as Mintzberg pointed out:

> Effective strategists are not people who abstract themselves from the daily detail but quite the opposite: they are the ones who immerse themselves in it, while being able to abstract the strategic messages from it. Perceiving the forest from the trees is not the right metaphor at all, therefore, because opportunities tend to be hidden under the leaves. A better one may be to detect a diamond in the rough in a seam of ore. Or to mix the metaphors, no one ever found a diamond by flying over a forest. From the air, a forest looks like a simple carpet of green, not the complex living system it really is.[4]

The difficulty was to redefine the CEO's role as he carried it out so as to re-immerse him in the organisation, but at a higher level. Gareth Morgan notes that there are two styles of CEO:

> Most of the time you have someone who is extraordinarily capable of dealing with today's operations, or someone who is very capable of

> dealing with the vision. But it's rare that you have
> both in one person . . . I sometimes ask myself
> whether this has something to do with our love for
> the pyramidal structure . . . To be a visionary and a
> day-to-day man is rare.[5]

The CEO in this Study was both. However, Morgan
goes on to underline the importance of involving the
whole organisation in the strategic process:

> You have to get as many people in the organisation
> as possible blending today and tomorrow in their
> approach to day-to-day management. It's not just
> something that the CEO should do. It should go
> right down the organisation. There is not a discon-
> tinuity between today and tomorrow.[6]

For the senior management, the Study suggested two-
fold benefits in participation in the strategic process:
not only would the quality of their decision-making be
raised by a deeper understanding of the underlying
goals and means, but the results of the process itself
would be enriched by their involvement. As Bartlett
and Ghoshal pointed out:

> The problem is not the CEO but rather the as-
> sumption that the CEO *should* be the corporation's
> chief strategist, assuming full control of setting the
> company's objectives and determining its priori-
> ties. In an environment where the fast-changing
> knowledge and expertise required to make such
> decisions are usually found at the front lines, this
> assumption is untenable.[7]

There is another distinction — between individuals
who take a long view and those who live for today.

And as they get older those characteristics are reinforced. I have seen good "gee-I'm-glad-to-meet-you"
salesmen get bored stiff at discussions about the future,
even about next month's budget. We should not let notions of participation land us with participants who
have nothing to contribute to the strategic process.[8]

Although in principle all senior management should
be involved in the process, in practice the close strategic
group needs to be carefully chosen. I agree with Bates
and Dillard, when they argue that:

> Experience and research have clearly demon-
> strated that (1) success as an operational line man-
> ager or (2) attaining a high position in the
> organisational hierarchy is not a valid indication of
> the possession of the capability to think strategi-
> cally. Research also indicates that successful stra-
> tegic thinking is related to certain measurable
> capabilities, such as intuitive ability, mental elas-
> ticity, abstract thinking, tolerance of risk, and tol-
> erance for ambiguity. However, identification of
> the strategic thinkers is made difficult by the ne-
> cessity to determine two critical aspects: ability
> and disposition (motivation), as reflected by cer-
> tain personality traits such as ambition and social
> skills. Thus, a firm must not only find the indi-
> viduals with the ability to think strategically but
> also identify a disposition or motivation to use the
> strategic thinking capability.
>
> Therefore, the crucial task of selecting the strategic
> planning group members is not one that can be ful-
> filled by *carte blanche* appointment of the executive
> staff to the strategic planning group. To do so is
> tantamount to ensuring the failure of the strategic
> planning group except in those rare instances

when the executive staff also have the ability and
motivation to be strategic thinkers.[9]

This was the first Study, and it is evident that the mel-
lower attitude noted in the *Introduction* has not set in.
The apocalyptic turn of phrase — "a tendency for the
organisation to fall apart", no less — recalls some gurus, exemplified by the quality expert W.E. Deming,
who was wont to finish his presentation by saying:
"You don't have to accept my ideas. Survival isn't
compulsory." The organisation did not, of course, fly
apart, as will be seen in the 1988/89 Study (No. 4 below).

The laconic conclusion — "Plans are important.
Planning is critical." — presents an idea that *has* en-
dured and has been developed in the Studies below.
That is, the benefits of the planning process, if carefully
entered into, far outweigh the benefits of the resultant
plan, though this itself is valuable.

Notes

1. The Kami manual referred to is a detailed strategic process in
   handbook form, devised by Michael Kami, consultant and
   author.

2. Henry Mintzberg (1987), "The Strategy Concept 1: Five Ps for
   Strategy", *California Management Review*", Autumn, p. 21.

3. F.A. Maljers (1990), "Strategic Planning and Intuition in Unilever", *Long-Range Planning*, Vol. 23, No. 2, pp. 63 and 64.

4. Henry Mintzberg (1994), *The Rise and Fall of Strategic Planning*, London: Prentice Hall, pp. 256–7.

5. Gareth Morgan (1987), *Riding the Cutting-Edge of Change*, York University: Faculty of Administrative Studies, p. 101.

6. Gareth Morgan, *op. cit.*, p. 101.

7. Christopher A. Bartlett and Sumantra Ghoshal (1994), "Beyond Strategy to Purpose", *Harvard Business Review*, November–December, p. 81.

8. See: Gabriele Morello (ed.) (1994), *Time Perception in Marketing and Social Research*, Proceedings of the ISIDA Seminar, 18–20 May, Palermo: ISIDA.

9. D.L. Bates and John E. Dillard, Junior (1993), "Generating Strategic Thinking Through Multi-Level Teams", *Long Range Planning*, Vol. 26, No. 5, p. 103.

Chapter 5

STUDY 2 (1986):
A STATE COMPANY FACING COMPETITION

INTRODUCTION

In 1986, I had my first assignment with a State company. Having been chairman of a State company for seven years and knowing many State company chief executives in the IMI, I had sympathy with their unique problems. The barons of old were now gone, the men who had headed up the State companies in their pioneering days: J.F. Dempsey of Aer Lingus (who told politicians to their astonishment that canvassing would automatically disqualify a job applicant); Tod Andrews of Bord na Móna, CIE and Radio Telefís Éireann (who, since he had been out with a parabellum in the Troubles would tell ministers when *he* would see *them*); and the legendary Tim O'Driscoll of the Tourist Board (who had a chauffeur-driven Jaguar with the registration number 777 from which he would emerge in a cloud of Havana smoke as the chauffeur held the door. He died on 23 October 1998 in his 91st year. I am sure he is enjoying a celestial cigar.) It may well have been he who drew on the State company chief executives the envy of the bureaucracy and led to the pernicious Red Devlin Report which locked the State CEOs into a humiliating salary pecking order which market forces are only now beginning to break through.

The CEO who commissioned this Study had come from private enterprise and felt more acutely than most the constraints of the State sector and of an imposed board of directors. His objective was to make a business of the business.

There were 20 participants.

DIAGNOSIS: SUMMARY OF PARTICIPANTS' VIEWS

It is almost a truism to describe competitiveness in a changing market as, objectively, the key issue in this Study. Subjectively, it was widely enough perceived as the key issue. But the strength of that perception, and the degree of concern about it, varied considerably depending on the individual's job and current preoccupation.

In the Chairman's Annual Review of 1985, it was said that the company was "moving towards its stated strategy of being a marketing-pulled operation rather than production-pushed as in the past". It was doubtful if many managers saw the company that way. Sir Colin Marshall opined:

> Marketing practices have limited power in themselves when they're not supported by the corporate culture. The distinction is between ritual and commitment: marketing practices work best where they emerge from a deep, comprehensive com-

mitment to the market. For instance, time spent by the chief executive with customers appears to be linked positively with business performance. This research [conducted by the London Business School] is building up one of the most convincing pieces of evidence in favour of market-based business strategy. It demonstrates that a strong external focus is critical to success.

In management literature we often see innovation praised and extolled. But innovation is not abstract; it has to be forged out of a concrete set of circumstances. I believe that the root of most innovation comes from the supplier–customer interface, not the lab. The most innovative companies are the ones that listen and that don't feel threatened or defensive about criticism.

If those of us who head companies don't keep our customers in sight and earshot all the time, we deserve to be passed over. This challenges the status quo and many firms where production and finance have the upper hand. To succeed in today's environment, customers have to be brought out of the back room and put front and centre in every aspect of business activity.[1]

In general, the company was perceived as being product-pushed because of the nature of its operations: of being to a considerable extent in the commodity market, where the single most significant factor was price; of being very vulnerable (unlike in the past) to international competition. The inherited burden of debt was seen as something (a) nobody believed the company could trade out of, and (b) which inhibited access to the capital needed for competitiveness.

There was a good deal of sympathy, and little scapegoating, of the marketing people, who were perceived as having a difficult task.

There was some concern that, particularly during the then current joint venture negotiations, marketing was not much discussed and its problems not widely shared throughout the company.

REMEDY: SUMMARY OF PARTICIPANTS' VIEWS

In the *Interim Report*, the Chairman's statement that the company was "moving towards its stated strategy of being marketing-pulled rather than production-pushed" got little support. In the *Planning Report*, there was a shift. While many people still saw the company as being in the commodity business, with price as the major marketing factor, there was increasing awareness of the efforts of the marketing people — who saw one of their first jobs as to sell themselves *inside* the company.

The *Interim Report* noted some concern about the fact that marketing was not much discussed during the joint venture negotiations. That concern was still there, but was reinforced by a strong perception that marketing decisions (in particular) had been long-fingered during the negotiations, with consequent loss of ground to competitors.

Closely related to this was the view that the company was a soft mark, not sufficiently aggressive when aggressiveness was called for in marketing or in negotiations with competitors.

While, interestingly, a lot of the discussion about competitiveness in the second interviews focused on marketing, there was a widespread view that competitiveness was all-embracing.

There were probably three main strands in views about greater productive efficiency:

1. That reducing manpower costs was something that would go on forever;

2. That the company had almost reached the end of the road in rationalisations, was weary of the obsession with them and should now encourage better morale and teamwork by having done with them; and

3. That further major advances in productivity could be got only by major capital expenditure.

Here, the consciousness of the inherited burden of debt was evident. This led to some differing views. On the one hand, there was a feeling of achievement in increased efficiencies; on the other, a feeling that no matter how fast we ran, we would not get much farther forward.

Quality was mentioned a few times, but not often.

The weight of the numbers of production people in the company versus the marketing people was seen as significant.

There was a view that market share was a, if not the, key indicator and that this was not sufficiently realised in the past, with a consequent sluggish marketing response.

There was almost unanimous agreement that there was no overall strategy for the company.

The result was that decisions were seen as being taken in isolation, in no strategic context, or, probably worse, that no decisions were being taken at all, while competitors manoeuvred.

The principal cause of this was seen as:

1. The CEO's preoccupation with a joint venture; and

2. His personally leading those negotiations.

There was some feeling that thinking was sequential, i.e., that one thing could not be decided until another thing was fixed, and that the world was not like that: an enterprise had to move on several fronts at the same time. In this way, opportunities were missed and the quality of decision-making was reduced because it was one-track, blinkered.

It was felt that strategy was the primary responsibility of the CEO and executive committee. There was scant sympathy for the idea of a corporate planner other than the chief executive.

The following verbatim views show the participants' concerns about a State company facing growing competition:

> "Competitiveness is the end result of doing everything as right as possible."

"It is very hard to be conscious of being market-pulled: 80 per cent of managers are in production."

"Decisions are needed on what market we go for."

"Three to four years ago, competitiveness meant getting costs right. After that, competitiveness means strategy — doing the right things. We are at the point of diminishing returns for further competitiveness. The real emphasis was on first line managers in the past. That's been done. Now up the line to strategy."

"It would take a sustained level of reasonably good prices to fight our way out of where we are. And if you do make the money, the government will be in for its pound of flesh, so there is no investment."

"We are taking fire-fighting action, getting as lean as we can. We have to have our fixed costs as low as you can. But if the market place continues as difficult, you won't be substantially better off."

"We are not self-confident in our approach to the market. We have consistently lost market share."

"We should stop being nice guys. We are afraid to hurt other people. Some of this is traditional. It should have changed. We don't have the balls for it. There's always a reason for not being tough. It demands a lot of change. We are probably afraid. If we hit a guy, he might hit us back."

"The marketing people have got a lot of stick over the years. However, the marketing function is now communicating better. The marketing liaison meetings are working well. If Ivor Kenny's work was done two years ago, he might have been told the problem was marketing."

"Marketing is a commercial activity — we are not market-led. Good commercial management is what's needed. Also, you have got to sell yourself to the rest of the company. And the marketing men have to sell the company. Therefore, they must sell themselves first inside. There has been progress on this."

"Competitiveness means being a whole company committed to its objectives. At present, we are taking aspects of the company and raising them to the level of the total company. There has to be a balance. You can be totally uncompetitive with an uncompetitive workforce. They are just as important as technical problems."

"We deal only with aspects of competitiveness. Unless we are careful in the way we proceed about competitiveness, it will blow up in our face."

"Marketing has not been discussed *broadly* enough. It is dealt with only in a small conclave."

"We have to be aggressive at times, accommodating at times. The time to be aggressive is when your opponent is weak. Sometimes it's not enough to say you are going to do something."

"We are perceived as a soft mark."

"The search for efficiency has no end."

"If you want capital expenditure, you want a shareholder who can take a long view."

"The company has made tremendous efforts. We are obsessed with reductions. There is an over-emphasis on getting rid of people. Maybe now is the time to look up. If I were operations manager I would be resisting further rationalisations."

ADVISER'S PRESENT (1998) COMMENTARY

This Study was the least successful of the Studies undertaken. There were two reasons.

The first was in the methodology. There was no concluding conference, no closure. All I had was a one-hour slot in a management conference at which three other "items" were considered and where there was even a guest speaker. This was despite the great good will of the chief executive towards the Study.

The second reason, far more important, was timing. A degree of calm, of normalcy, of stability is necessary to enter a company. I dislike the cliché "turbulence" but it serves to describe a condition in which people find it difficult to take a semi-detached view. They are preoccupied with the problems of the here-and-now. The chief executive was preoccupied with a possible merger which would, and subsequently did, change the nature of the company — and give him expanded freedom to manoeuvre.

The analysis of the shortcomings in the company — an analysis, it must be reiterated, done by the participants themselves — was accurate.

But to criticise the chief executive for focusing almost exclusively on the merger is to stretch beyond practicality theories about comprehensive strategic planning. There are times when a narrow or, more benignly, a focused vision is essential to make things happen.

This driving focus was explored in my study of entrepreneurs.[2]

Entrepreneurs see the opportunity in a way that probably defies objective analysis. They know what is right and go for it. They may become impatient with "rational" arguments from their colleagues which go against their convictions. They may characterise contrary arguments in emotional terms as lacking guts or vision — though they are canny enough to foresee pitfalls which they may or may not deliberately choose to ignore. They will likely leave a trail of unattended matters in their drive towards their goal — if we were to get everything right (an impossibility anyway) before taking action, we would never get anywhere. They believe the more mundane job of management, as distinct from creative leadership, can be left till later.

These Studies are mainly about the mundane job of management. But they are certainly not about inhibiting the entrepreneurial urge.

It is, therefore, critical that, before undertaking a Study, the adviser has a clear read of the organisation and that he is not going into a situation where the ground will shift in the course of the Study. The analysis of the management issues may be right, as they were in this Study. The circumstances in which that analysis could be given practical effect may be lacking.

Notes

1. Sir Colin Marshall, quoted in: William Dauphinais and Colin Price (eds.) (1998), *Straight from the CEO: The World's Top Business Leaders Reveal Ideas that Every Manager Can Use*, London: Nicolas Brealey Publishing, p. 139.

2. Ivor Kenny (1987), *Out on Their Own*, Dublin: Gill and Macmillan, p. 8: "What finally distinguishes entrepreneurs from other people is that, whatever their beliefs about luck, about timing and about being in the right place at the right time, they are the ones who see the opportunities and who do something about them."

3. See also the following:

   P.M. Kilby (1971), *Entrepreneurship and Economic Development*, New York: The Force Press, p. 27; Chad Perry (1990), "After Further Sightings of the Heffalump", *Journal of Managerial Psychology*, Vol. 5, No. 2, pp. 22–31.

   Warren Bennis and Bert Nanus (1985), *Leaders*, New York: Harper & Row, p. 20.

   J.A. Timmons, L.E. Smollen and A.L.M. Dingee (1977), *New Venture Creation*, Homewood, IL: Irwin, *passim*.

   Mark Casson (1982), *The Entrepreneur: an Economic Theory*, Oxford: Martin Robertson, p. 11. Casson went on to define the entrepreneur as "someone who specialises in taking judgmental decisions about the co-ordination of scarce resources" (p. 23). *That did not get me anywhere at all.*

   J.W. Carland, F. Hoy, W.R. Boulton and J.A.C. Carland (1984), "Differentiating Entrepreneurs from Small Business Owners: a Conceptualisation", *Academy of Management Review*, Vol. 9, No. 2, pp. 354–9: "An entrepreneur is an individual who establishes and manages a business for the principal purposes of profit and growth. The entrepreneur is characterised principally by innovative behaviour and will employ strategic management practices in the business." *Carland told us what in his view the entrepreneur did. His definition did not purport to tell us why the entrepreneur did it and it would be stretching things to say that all entrepreneurs used strategic management practices – in my experience several of them cheerfully made things up as they went along.*

A.L. Carsrud, K.W. Olm and G.G. Eddy (1986), "Entrepreneurship: Research in Quest of a Paradigm", in D.L. Sexton and R.W. Smilor (eds.), *The Art and Science of Entrepreneurship*, Cambridge, MA: Ballinger, p. 368: "An entrepreneur is an individual who is willing and able to engage in personal risk-taking and responsibility, while at the same time combining the means of production and credit in the expectation of realizing profit and/or other specific objectives such as power and prestige." *We were getting close.*

G.G. Meredith, R.E. Nelson and P.A. Neck (1982), *The Practice of Entrepreneurship*, Geneva: International Labour Office, p. 3.

E. Chell (1986), "The Entrepreneurial Personality: a Review and Some Theoretical Developments" in J. Curran *et al.* (eds.), *The Survival of the Small Firm, Volume 1: The Economics of Survival and Entrepreneurship*, Aldershot: Gower, pp. 102–19.

Elizabeth Chell and Jean M. Haworth (1988), *Explorations of the Entrepreneurial Personality*, Paper presented to the Second Workshop on Recent Research on Entrepreneurship, European Institute for Advanced Studies in Management, Vienna, 5–6 December.

Mark Casson, *The Entrepreneur: an Economic Theory*, Oxford: Martin Robertson, 1982, p. 11.

Joyce O'Connor and Mary Lyons (1983), *Enterprise – The Irish Approach*, Dublin: The Industrial Development Authority, Publication Series Paper 7. *Also* M.P. Fogarty, *Irish Entrepreneurs Speak for Themselves*, Dublin: ESRI Broadsheet No. 8, December, 1973.

John A. Murray (1981), "In Search of Entrepreneurship", *Journal of Irish Business and Administrative Research*, p. 3, pp. 43 *et seq.*; Patrick O'Farrell (1986), *Entrepreneurs and Industrial Change: the Process of Change in Irish Manufacturing*, Dublin: Irish Management Institute.

See Chad Perry, *op cit.*, p. 27: "The major characteristic distinguishing entrepreneurs from the general population and other groups is not a personality trait like risk-taking propensity, but a perception of the relevant risk in the world; that is, the distinguishing characteristic is not an approach or reaction to the world, it is how the world is perceived."

Chapter 6

STUDY 3 (1987):
THE NEED FOR PARTICIPATION

INTRODUCTION

Study 3 was an Irish subsidiary of a global corporation producing and selling high-quality branded products. It had a strong culture, was conscious of its historic origins and acutely sensitive to the marketplace. To illustrate: because they were selling a high-quality product, there was a strict dress code. I was walking along a corridor with the CEO when we met a young marketing executive. He was wearing a beautifully cut double-breasted blazer, dark flannels, a white shirt and sober tie. I thought he looked very smart. The CEO said, "Murphy, are you going on a picnic?"

My entry to the company was through long conversations with the chief executive about his own role. He commanded much deserved respect but had become aloof. His private report was critical of him. At the final conference he said,

> "Now I've learned a lot about myself through this Study, maybe things I might prefer not to know. But it's good that I do know, and Ivor, I think can

confirm that I have taken a positive attitude to
most, if not all, of the criticisms."

Twenty senior managers took part in the Study.

DIAGNOSIS (THE *INTERIM REPORT*)

There was concern that the Group did not have a clear,
widely shared, comprehensive strategy or a strategic
capacity.

There was some concern about dependency on one
product.

REMEDY

In the *Interim Report* it was noted that Strategy was "put
as the first priority, based not entirely on a consensus
that that is where it should be, but influenced by the
adviser's view that everything else depends on it". No
such reservation was necessary with the second interviews. Two-thirds of the participants chose it as the
number one priority (and of the remaining seven participants, four chose it as number two).

There was agreement that:

- There was no Group strategic process, even if some
  of the views in the *Interim Report* were regarded as
  too strong;

- The need for wide and genuine participation in that
  process was emphasised;

- A gap between planning and action was seen.

In broad summary, the participants were saying that *the Group* and its constituent companies needed a *strategic capacity* in which *managers shared*.

There were many specific suggestions about what should be done. The following selection of verbatim views give the flavour of them:

> "The company must foster and encourage strategic thinking about our business, future environment, competitors, etc. as a continuous process."

> "The process must be multidisciplinary."

> "The process must involve all levels of management."

> "The process must assume high priority and resources: time, facilities, money must be forthcoming."

> "We should have a more consistent commitment to a given strategy — say three years. Get the implementation of this strategy correct from day one."

> "A five-year strategic plan is prepared each year. This should be communicated to key managers, seeking input from them."

> "Strategy suggests a long-term plan. It seems to me that it is the plan that is missing rather than the will to strategise."

> "Strategy in the company is more gut feel for the future."

> "1. We should identify the need for:
>   - overall strategy;

- individual company strategy.

"We should identify the options, establish priorities and strategies.

"The way in which this can be done interrelates with the areas of style and communications and culture. And the identification of the priorities also interrelates with these other areas.

"2. The Board should give full and serious consideration to its role in the company, particularly from a strategic point of view and, if it accepts that strategy is fundamental, then give it priority."

"The Board requires the support of a small group of senior managers with direct access to it to assist in anticipating change in trends, and assisting in decision-making and strategy."

"1. Develop the company's mission statement: Why are we in business? It should be simple, concise, measurable and sacred for one year.

"2. We should define the departmental roles — production, marketing, finance etc.

"3. We should define departmental strategies consisting of three elements: (a) objective statement; (b) strategy — how will we reach objective; (c) operating guidelines.

"The latter two must be developed by departmental management, not imposed.

"These would be the elements in formulating an overall company strategy."

"A strategy committee should be set up, chaired by the CEO, with representatives from each division and department, not just the Board of directors, but also, for example, a representative from production. There should be specific people to sit on the committee.

"It should meet every three months to review existing strategy and to discuss emerging strategy. This meeting would be day-long, and involve the strategy of the entire business, not just the marketing strategy. This may also have the benefit of solving some of the communications problems, where some of the managers don't know what other managers are doing or planning to do."

"We must be consistent in any form of strategy adopted. Strategy should be a shared, clear and totally agreed company philosophy."

"Just as the business plan contains the annual budgets, on which the company's performance is judged in the following year, and since the budgets are a distillation of management input — can we not put together an annual review of strategy by management? We need an annual management session where the basic strategic plans are formulated, with input from all senior managers and reviewed on a rollover basis annually as conditions alter. In essence, management needs to play a greater role in formulating the business plan rather than just having a budgetary input as at present."

"The company's strategy should be a shared and co-ordinated document."

"The current strategy is formulated from the point of view of the Board. What about opportunities and influences and trends which are developing in areas about which the Board may not know?"

"We should create an organisation framework for setting strategy. There should be a contribution from all senior executives to strategy decisions. This is essential. The strategy should cover short, medium, and long term. There should be a network for the execution of missions — clear and with built-in checks."

"Lay the concern to rest. The CEO should communicate what the company strategy is, and open it up for comment. It is important that this task is performed by the CEO."

"The chief executive plus the Board should be more active in evolving strategy and less active in operational matters. Strategy should be regularly reviewed, updated and communicated to senior managers.

- Develop a vision for the future.

- Strive to be on the leading edge of new trends.

- Avoid short-term orientation and low-risk strategies.

- Use research intelligently to inform successful strategies.

- Live in the longer term.

- Create the future.

- Focus on implementing what needs to be changed.

- Foster deep commitment to strategic thinking from which the strategy will be developed.

- Ensure that strategy is followed wholeheartedly.

- We must satisfy customer/consumer needs.

- We need to be pre-emptive.

- Capitalise on our strengths.

- Anticipate change.

- Be sensitive to people's needs."

ADVISER'S COMMENTARY (1987)

A Strategic Capacity

The chief executive is the chief strategist. This is one job that cannot be delegated. (The appointment of a "corporate planner", except in very large enterprises, is frequently evidence of a failure genuinely to plan.) The chief executive will need around him a Strategic Planning Group representative of the various elements in the organisation, e.g., marketing, finance, HR, production, R&D, DP. Each element will have a sub-group to ensure that adequate information is available. The Strategic Planning Group will have a definite system of work:

- to ensure an orderly and comprehensive approach to its task;

- to ensure that deadlines are met;

- to ensure a free flow of communication up and down;

- to ensure that the process is protected, i.e., that the urgent does not drive out the important.

To this end, meetings would be set at the beginning of the year and changed only to facilitate the process — not to accommodate some short-term priority.

Sharing

With many managers sharing in the process, there are several benefits. Firstly, there is an increase in morale. Managers feel listened to, feel part of the organisation, feel they can influence decisions in which they have a particular expertise. Secondly, the quality of decision-making is improved because of adequate technical input from levels where the technical knowledge is sharpest. Thirdly, "everyone sings from the same hymn-book": the components in the organisation move in the same direction; the organisation should recognise, respond quickly and consistently to new threats and opportunities without constant checking from the top; the organisation feels more secure in its grip on the future — rumour and speculation, which waste energy, are minimised. Fourthly, there is greater energy. People carry out with enthusiasm only recommendations in whose formulation they have participated.

The Study showed — as it was designed to when the chief executive commissioned it — the level of understanding of the issues facing the company and the level of commitment to resolving them. This was reinforced by the quality of the reports at a concluding conference.

In closing that session, the chief executive said that the reports would be listened to and acted upon.

If certain key actions are taken, others have to follow and, hopefully, the many issues raised in the Study will then be addressed.

The first necessary step is

To Establish a Strategic Planning Process

The characteristics of the process are well covered in the *Report*. It must begin with a (not immutable) mission statement from the chief executive and be

- Comprehensive

- Continuous, and

- Participative.

ADVISER'S PRESENT (1998) COMMENTARY

This was a company which had produced a world-beating product. Success has many fathers, but much of the credit must be given to the chief executive, an unreconstructed marketing man who was seen as autocratic.

The participants' conclusions on strategy are good textbook stuff. They were, however, expressing a need deeper than participating in strategy formulation: a need to know and understand where the company was going, where they fitted in and where they could apply

their expertise to things which, in their view, were being done wrong.

(The Study had an unforeseen and beneficial side effect, not referred to above. Having produced one enduring world-beater, they wanted to produce a second
one, to which they were devoting time and energy.
They found they were better off forgetting about that
chimera and devoting all their energy to developing
their existing product, which has today, in its niche,
become as unassailable as any world product can be.)

The main theme of this work is being reinforced:
that a shared strategic process precedes, and in may
ways is more important than, a strategy.

However, looking back now, my "commentary" was
a bit prescriptive, neat and tidy. As Warner and Arnold
remark:

> This higgledy-piggledy growth of theory presents
> great problems to managers and to those who ad-
> vise them about the best way to carry out strategic
> planning in their organisations . . . In some cases it
> may be felt that a structured approach along the
> lines of Ansoff's and Argenti's thinking may be
> right. For instance, the SWOT phase, analysing the
> organisation and its environment, can incorporate
> a BCG matrix and/or a Porter industry analysis. A
> PIMS analysis can also be part of the appraisal. The
> mission statement and the evaluation of strategic
> options must face the crucial issues of diversifica-
> tion raised by Levitt and confront the question of
> acquisition versus organic growth . . . It is danger-
> ous to assume that this kind of sequential proce-
> dure is necessarily right for all organisational
> cultures. Organisations who consider that they

> need help to formalise their planning procedures
> may in fact be developing strategy very effectively
> in their own informal ways . . . The common
> thread which is vital to all these planning ap-
> proaches is that they must all lead to implementa-
> tion and must result in personal responsibility for
> action with deadlines.[1]

Perhaps I tended to minimise the uniquely creative role of the chief executive. His conviction and persistence made the company what it was. Formal planning may impede strategic thinking.[2] Sometimes strategies emerge. Sometimes a precedent is set, a decision taken, which sets a direction without being identified as such. Sometimes strategies can be imposed by the environment. And sometimes they come from a single charismatic leader, as was true in this instance.

Perhaps the organisation's search for a second world-beating product was *his* search, *à la recherche du temps perdu*.

Notes

1. Alan Warner and David Arnold (1986), "Navigating the Strategic Maze", *Management Decision*, Vol. 24, No. 6, pp. 25–44.

2. Author's notes on Henry Mintzberg address to the Third Annual Strategic Management Society Conference, 26–29 October 1983, Paris.

Chapter 7

STUDY 4 (1988/89): CULTURE, STYLE AND CAPABILITY

INTRODUCTION

This company was also the subject of the 1985 Study. In three years it had changed from an Irish to an international company and was moving from commodity to value-added branded goods.

The final objective of every Study is stated as a clear, shared strategy, or, as we see increasingly, a strategic capacity. It will be seen from what follows that that is what this Study ended with, but the approach was more complex, less straightforward, than the previous Studies.

The chief executive's concern was expressed in characteristically blunt manner: "They're not coming up." The company was growing rapidly in scope, turnover and profits. He believed that management capability was not keeping pace, particularly at middle management level.

An outside observer at that time might say the managers were not coming up because the chief executive would not let them. He was a dominant, charismatic

and visionary chief executive. Because of the performance of his company, he attracted an amount of publicity. It gave to those who did not know the organisation
an impression of a one-man-band. But he admitted to
me, "The people around here ask me questions to
which I often have no answers."

A moment's thought would be sufficient to understand that a large, complex organisation, that doubled
in size in three years, could not be run by a one-man-
band. The first job for the Study was to identify the organisational blockages to the growth of managers.
What emerged was that those blockages lay within the
organisation's culture, style, capability and lack of
(systematic) management development.

For these interrelated and complex reasons, this
Study is reported in some detail.

There were 53 participants: 21 senior managers (referred to in the Study as first-line) and 32 of their nomi-
nees (referred to as second-line). The Study showed
differences between them.

DIAGNOSIS: SUMMARY OF PARTICIPANTS' VIEWS

Culture

The company culture was a strong, recognisable one
with a tendency to see life in simple, "common sense",
terms.

The predominant characteristics of the culture were
loyalty, energy, adventurousness/risk-taking, pride,
buzz and discipline. While there were some differences

in perspective between first- and second-line managers, they were not significant.

Negative aspects were a closed culture, a sensitivity to outside criticism against an awareness that the company had not always done everything right.

> Because life is simplified by the *closing* of gates, a manager's first impulse may be to do just that — to close off new ideas or to direct them into well worn channels where they will be gradually eroded into recognisable, comfortable shapes. Yet to grow, organisations, like individuals, require the stimulus of challenge and innovation. That is, the management of these activities distinguishes organisations that learn from those that do not.[1]

The bottom line was seen, both by first- and second-line managers, as almost the reason for existing. It tended to put quality in the second place. It drove out thought: it was not a thoughtful organisation. Things were perceived as too tight, causing mistakes.

The culture was strong on managers being seen to work long hours. There was evidence of overload among the first-line managers. There was evidence of growing disenchantment among the second-line managers, though some had taken the problem in hand. A significant complaint was that they had no time to think.

The company was perceived as secretive. The first-line managers (who, presumably, were in on most major decisions) saw this primarily as insulating the company from developments in the world outside. The second-line managers saw it not only as keeping out information/knowledge but also as formally excluding them from company information, which they would learn informally (and maybe inaccurately) anyway.

Both first- and second-line managers saw the organisation as conformist, shading into compliance.

. There was some good-humoured pride in the belief that the company did things the hard way, i.e., not learning from the experience of others.

Style

First-line managers were results-driven. Second-line managers appreciated autonomy.

Some first-line managers saw the long-term dangers of a consistently autocratic style. While perceiving the company as traditionally autocratic, the second-line managers were ambivalent about the style: some saw dangers, others thought it was the way to run things.

Some first-line managers saw the management style as pressured and questioned whether the pressure led to better results. Second-line managers saw it as counterproductive.

First-line managers saw the company as poor on communicating, on letting people know what was going on, particularly from the top down. This view was shared, perhaps more strongly, by second-line managers.

The usefulness of away meetings as a forum of communication — or, more meaningfully, participation — was questioned by first-line managers.

There were some perceptions that you were as good — or as bad — as your last mistake.

Capability

While a high proportion of first-line managers could nominate a successor, there was a strong consensus among them that the company's management capability, without distinction of levels, was thin on the ground.

The concern (and consensus) was even stronger in the second-line. They saw an absolute shortage of good people. This was exacerbated by the propensity of the organisation (as they perceived it) to snatch people away to where top management believed there was a greater need.

We have noted that loyalty was highly valued. Loyalty/commitment were seen as prime ingredients in carrying the company through, in overcoming shortcomings in, or shortages of, managers — but there were warnings about how long that might last.

There was an acknowledgement that several jobs required, not high-fliers, but good soldiers.

There were the beginnings (from first-line managers only) of thoughts about what needed to be done. This would be the subject matter of the remedial stage of this Study.

Management Development

There was a concern among first-line managers about the unsystematic way management development was approached, a concern more or less shared by the second line.

Autonomy/delegation/management-by-leaving-them-alone was seen by the first-line managers as the key factor in developing managers on the job. (This contrasted with the autocratic style noted earlier.) The second-line managers would agree and saw development opportunities also in the growth of the company, in getting out to the market place, in variety in the job.

The first-line managers who offered views seemed to see the organisation as almost anti management training. The second-line managers would welcome management training, particularly in specific skills.

The first-line managers believed that the divisional managers should be held responsible for management development.

There was unanimity that annual reviews were a good thing, both for the reviewer and the reviewed, but were not done well throughout the organisation.

Some uncertainty about what management development actually involved was expressed by the first-line managers. Perceived barriers, including this uncertainty, were that:

- It was low on the list of priorities — lack of real interest, other pressures;

- There was no tolerance of "spare" people;

- Real determination from the top was lacking;

- There was an unwillingness to share staff between divisions;

- There was — at least up to then — no manpower planning.

Second-line views on barriers were that:

- Doing was driving out developing;

- The culture was sink-or-swim;

- You got no thanks for developing people; there was no receptive ear for managers' development needs;

- Management development was abstract, hard to measure;

- There was some stagnation, some managers involved in menial tasks;

- There was no money for management development.

Strategy

There was an awareness in the first-line of the risks in the organisation's fast-growth strategy. At the second-line level, insofar as risks were commented on, the necessity for growth was accepted.

Innovation was seen as coming from being close to the market, adding value and developing new products. The greatest brake on new products was seen as the difficulty to get money to do it.

At the first-line, there was some questioning of the quality of strategic thinking — and of the ability of some managers to think strategically. This was echoed by the second-line.

There were first-line views (here and elsewhere in the *Report*) that divisions needed an adequate level of capital development just to sustain their funding of acquisitions. Comments tended to focus on those divisions that felt beleaguered. The second-line would agree.

At either level, though perhaps more so at second-line, little synergy between divisions was seen. There was an implicit request for more collegiality on strategy formulation.

REMEDY: SUMMARY OF PARTICIPANTS' VIEWS

During the second interviews, the first-line managers agreed to give written reactions for incorporation in the *Report*. They were asked to concentrate on what should be done. Here they are drawn together and summarised, with the emphasis where possible on what should be done rather than on commentary.

Culture

The dominant view was that the culture should not be changed. One manager said it would serve the company better than "any unnatural type of culture". The point was made again, as it was made in the *Interim Report*, that there were many original and admirable components of the culture — and they must be fostered. Also, that there was no right or wrong culture or style, just what fitted and what the organisation was comfortable with.

On the one hand, it was stated that it was hard to keep confidential matters quiet if they were discussed with too many people; while, on the other, participants in the Study seemed to be feeling a degree of isolation.

There was support for the results-driven culture, "the bottom line": "The company is results-driven and long may that continue." The managers themselves should generate the emphasis on the bottom line by a proper appraisal system. A divisional manager said unequivocally, "My job is to attain the target set." However, a participant said that bottom-line emphasis, while a definite short-term benefit, was potentially dangerous long-term.

There were other views. The culture had served well but was not likely to succeed in the future. The organisation needed more quality thinking — but one participant said the organisation must have been thoughtful or it would not have got to where it was. The ideas and passions of the founding fathers might not impress graduates of the late 1980s. The top management should rely less on energy and more on thoughtfulness. It was felt that a variation on the culture might have to be accepted and that recruits from other businesses could bring in new thinking.

In summary, there was a fairly high degree of satisfaction with the culture and, therefore, no change but some voices suggested that change could be beneficial.

Style, including Communications

It was said that the company worked best under an autocratic style but that some managers expected the organisation to be a democracy when "they had more than adequate knowledge of the issues concerning their particular job".

Divisions had all the autonomy they wanted. It was the major task of the divisional manager to make sure the first and second levels of management made use of their autonomy.

Strategy, which had hardly been discussed in the *Interim Report* (though it was the major issue of the 1985 *Report*), came up a number of times. It was felt that the formalised corporate planning process would help clear up ambiguities; that the company needed a top-down strategic plan; that getting more of the key management involved in formulating strategies was vital; that the divisions had clear short-term goals and that the chief executive should get involved once a year at divisional level on long-term planning.

A participant said he could not see how people felt the company was poor on communicating. The view was that divisional managers did not have to know everything that was happening in other divisions; they had more than enough to do on their own. The away meetings should continue. All the troops should have discussions with the CEO's office in the course of the year. The office should make sure that they were sufficiently aware of first- and second-line views so as to eliminate the need for future Studies of this kind.

Capability

There were some bullish views on capability — at variance with the consensus in the *Interim Report*: "While we may be thin on the ground, we have a better calibre of individual"; "I strongly disagree with the suggestion that we have not been recruiting the best candidates — they represent the top end"; "Do we have difficulty getting a job elsewhere? The opposite is the case."

There were suggestions about hiring in some experienced managers.

There was concern about the second-line managers' lack of successors.

Management Development

One of the themes emerging from this Study — that management development is the responsibility of the divisional managers — was reinforced. There was the suggestion that the office of a management development executive should be abolished and divisional managers evaluated on their performance in developing people. There was now a commitment to management development.

Management development was a perennial issue — unsystematic, but it had worked well.

A participant said it was the critical issue, but the organisation's preoccupation with the short term was running against it. It needed to be systematic, formalised, a corporate *sine qua non*. Another said it was crucial to survival/success.

A five-year plan (presumably incorporating a man-power plan) was needed before people were developed. There was no point in developing people to a level above which the organisation needed them unless there were definite future openings. However, another participant made the point that there was not an infinite number of promotional opportunities and that there was an immense amount of personal development to be got on the job.

It was said that it was not practicable to transfer people between divisions.

On specific actions, it was suggested that the next wave of divisional managers now be identified and trained, that a key issue was to improve creativity in the marketing and technical areas, and that there should be at least one outside management training course a year to expose managers with potential to new, unbiased ideas. The informal management development should now be balanced with training in specific skills.

Should there be a budget for management development?

There was support for the current introduction of assessments, one participant saying they must be persevered with as the best form of management development. The training needs of the individual should be matched to needs as defined in the manpower plan. Managers should set goals for themselves as part of the annual review.

ADVISER'S FIRST COMMENTARY (1989)

Introduction

The analysis summarised above, taken together with the volume of data in the *Interim Report*, is a comprehensive self-assessment. It is a sign of the robust health of the company.

Relative to where it has come from in a short space of years, and by any Irish comparison, the company has been outstanding. It has blazed trails in which others are following. As any company manager would say, "We must have been doing something right."

The fact that it has been doing many things right has given the company the self-confidence to look at itself to see what might be improved and what might be impeding any improvement — or change.

It is almost trite to say that the culture, style and structures of the company which suited it so well in the past will not suit it equally well in the future. Yet that very statement, unless it is immediately followed by determined action, can appear threatening or cynical.

People do not resist change. They resist uncertainty. Until such time as the company can demonstrate to itself better ways to manage its affairs, there will always be regression to the old ways, to the tried and the true. Why should there not be when "new" ways are dimly understood because they have not been tried?

What blockages there are lie deep within the company's culture, which is a strong one. Culture is multifaceted. There cannot, therefore, issue from the Study a single clarion call. The company is too sophisticated to expect that. What will be required are different actions at different levels by different people. But these actions must stem from a conviction on the part of the chief executive and his immediate colleagues that changes are necessary. The changes will then require both persistence and experimentation — persistence when they don't work immediately, experimentation when they don't work at all.

The *Report* indicated what many of those changes might be: it gives an initial shopping list. Whether or not the organisation buys the items on the list will be a matter of choice by those who wield power. There is a fair indication of the ideas that might catch fire and of those that will sputter unless the flame is fanned.

The company knows that this adviser does not have much faith in prescriptive recommendations from outside consultants — better to help the company do its own diagnosis and decide on its own cure.

However, the Study was a learning experience. The adviser developed the following convictions en route. It would be wrong to suppress them. They are put forward as a framework.

Mission Statement

The company mission statement was:

> A major international corporation which will dominate the markets it serves through superior product quality and service to its customers, and the unique wholehearted commitment of every company employee.

This was a pretty clear mission statement and might form the point of departure. But it needed to be developed. The only one who could do that, or at least lead the process, was the chief executive.

Uncertainty is minimised when there is a grip on the future — a clear picture of what the company as a whole would look like in five years' time. Autonomy would increase and the need for close management diminish.

The mission statement could be developed by answering questions such as:

- What markets will we be in with what products?

- What present products will be obsolete?

- What countries will we have a physical presence in and what will be the likely management/divisional structure?

- What will the function of the company headquarters be, what will be central, what devolved, where will the headquarters be?

- What will be the key differences in the business(es) five years hence?

- What will be the principal financial/economic concerns and how will they be measured?

- What changes will there be in the environment(s) that will affect the company's competitive position? Competitors? Technology? Social, political and legislative? What environmental trends are visible now that can be extrapolated?

- What changes will there be in the influence that various stakeholders exert?

These questions were not, of course, comprehensive, but answering one would beg several others.

The process of developing the mission statement, if handled right, could be a powerful team-builder. With minimal backup, it need not take too much time.

Value Systems

Alongside this could go another process — that is, that the members of the chief executive's office make explicit their own value systems: what they really thought and felt about the Group and where they ultimately wanted it to go.

This was a condition precedent for any successful strategy formulation and, particularly, for the formulation of a manpower plan as a critical element in corporate strategy.

A Manpower Plan

A manpower plan was not just about numbers or about the company tidying up its act on recruitment, induction and promotion (tasks well signalled in the *Reports* and common currency for any professional management) but about the kind of people the company wanted for the future. The value system should clearly indicate what the chief executive's office thought about its managers. Did the company want, for example, managers who were open, flexible and responded to change in a timely fashion? Did it want sensitivity to the competitive environment? Did it want effective communicators, both internally and externally, to customers, competitors, interest groups? Did it want managers who could live comfortably with ambiguity? Did it want effective internal management under conditions of distributed power/alienation/differences in aspirations among employees? Did it want managers who could readily adapt to different countries and cultures? Did it want to be responsive to the personal needs/ambitions/aspirations of its employees? Did it want entrepreneurs? Did it want, within a shared vision, to encourage autonomy, independence, creativity?

The style and observable behaviour of top management are by far the strongest determinants of the culture of the company. That culture, as is abundantly clear from these *Reports*, is the key determinant of the company's capability.

If top management is concerned only with growth and not actively and personally with capability, then the company's capability will not match its aspirations. There are many jobs that can be delegated by the chief executive's office. There are some few that cannot. Capability is one of them. Strategy is the cool head of an organisation. Capability is its heart. They are inextricably linked.

Of course, capability will grow organically as the organisation grows. The problem is that organic — unplanned — growth may not be quick enough to meet the future.

THE CHIEF EXECUTIVE'S RESPONSE

(The following is a short summary of the chief executive's talk at the concluding conference of the Study.)

The Study suggests that each of us in particular as well as those around us should understand the written and the unwritten meaning of our mission statement. I will now put forward what it means to me. As I explain this, you may think we are aiming for the impossible. I still believe in what I said a few years ago, "Nothing should be looked at as being impossible: some things just take longer than others to work out."

Mission Statement

Let me now break down the mission statement:

1. *A major international organisation* — What countries? What products?

2. *Significant market shares internationally* — In which product areas?

3. *We shall dominate the markets we serve through superior product quality.*

4. *We shall dominate the markets we serve through superior service to our customers.*

5. *We shall dominate the markets we serve through the unique wholehearted commitment of every company employee.*

This mission statement would never have been written if it were not for the strong culture that characterises the organisation. The *Report* tells us what the positive aspects of the culture are. I would put the case that if it were not for these factors, we would not be leading the industry today, would not have a mission statement and ambition which aims for the stars in the years ahead.

If something needs to be done with the culture, it certainly is not that it be changed. However, it can be enhanced and improved as we have been doing as each year passes.

People and Planning

We do not need people in the absence of a plan. A plan is no use without the people to implement it. Success in the next five years will come from the two-pronged attack in these areas.

X has been named as the person with overall responsibility for the production of a five-year rolling plan. He liaises with divisions to ensure that the corporate gaps are met.

Y has responsibility to see that the manpower is there so that our missions, plans and targets can be implemented. *The organisation will move only at the speed of people development.* Y, being asked to take responsibility for this area, will, hopefully, rekindle all that we have learned about people in 15 years.

1. Our success has come from recruiting the best graduates and not keeping them around for too long if they cannot make it.

2. Our success has come from keeping the organisation young. It is important that good young people be identified, monitored, and moved quickly through the organisation.

3. Our culture, the will to win, is the best around. While we change and enhance it, let us grow more people in it.

4. Poor performing people should be got rid of as it lowers the overall standard.

5. Acquisitions, regardless of where they take place, will call for a number of our people to bring to those acquisitions our culture and discipline. This must be catered for in competence, in language, in youth and in enthusiasm.

6. Priority now is to recruit top graduates in the countries where we do business and to have them work side by side with their colleagues in Ireland before going back with our disciplines to their own countries.

7. More than anything else, we must recruit entrepreneurs and ensure that our organisation encourages rather than stifles their development.

8. As acquisitions are the cornerstone of our plan, we must always have available and trained enough low-cost production expertise, accountants who can quickly pinpoint what needs to be done, and hands-on people who can put it into place.

Culture

Planning and thought must be brought into our culture, not to replace what is there, but to enhance it. Contrary to the *Report*, people are not *asked* to work long, hard hours. People are expected to work the hours they are happy to give to the organisation. People are not rewarded for hours, they are rewarded for performance.

Our culture is one of "excellence". The means, not the end, is the only thing that needs enhancing.

Senior executives X and Y then gave a detailed outline of, respectively, the planning process, in the Argenti model, and management development about which executive Y said, "In summary, unless there is a realistic strategic planning process, it is doubtful that a process of human resource development will on its own bring about the level of change that may be required."

ADVISER'S SECOND COMMENTARY (1989)

When senior management met three-and-a-half years ago to discuss the 1985 Study, one group defined management development as follows:

> Management development is the conscious investment of time, money and effort in people to enable them to do their current jobs more effectively and to prepare them for fulfilling different and/or more responsible roles in the future.

> It is a fine balance between the objectives/needs of the company and the objectives/needs of the individual.

They defined the problems as follows:

- Delegation (about which managers can be ambivalent if they see subordinates as a threat)
- Succession (there is no second-line)
- Broadening of horizons (greater exposure to other organisations and breaking down internal boundaries)
- Acquisitions
- Insufficient sense of identity with the company.

They said that the need had been recognised for some years but the commitment had been lacking.

These were elegant definitions and diagnoses. They still apply. What, if anything, has changed?

Two things:

1. The company is to double in size and become a truly international corporation in the next five years — and the implications of this have now been clearly spelled out; and

2. The chief executive has pointed out that "the organisation will move only at the speed of people development" and the responsibility for human resources has been raised to the level of the chief executive's office (just as corporate planning has also been raised to that level).

Human resources development, manpower planning, management development, recruitment and assessment are, perhaps for the first time, being taken seriously in the sense that there is the beginning of a determination to manage them.

John Argenti defines corporate planning as "any systematic method of making long-term strategic decisions affecting the company as a whole".

Perhaps the single most consistent criticism of human resources management in the Study was that it was unsystematic — that is, unmanaged.

A careful comparison with the 1985 Study shows that there has been a significant increase in awareness of the problem and some development of ideas about what needs to be done.

There is also evidence of a healthy impatience with continuing talk about human resources and a felt need for decisions (the second key word in Argenti's definition). This adviser would concur and go further. If strategic decisions about human resources are not seen to be taken (and continually followed up), then the latent cynicism about the company's commitment to human resources will be reinforced. As was suggested at the conference, the answer is not to try to move on several fronts at once but to begin by doing well a number of things perceived as valued, such as recruitment, which is relatively easy, and assessments, which are harder.

The need for a management development "person", other than Y in the CEO's office, came to be almost taken for granted as the group-work progressed. The company would not dream of appointing a person at senior level until it was clear about what the company wanted him or her for, so that it could judge accurately the qualities and capabilities needed. This should apply to the human resources person. It is the adviser's view that more work needs to be done by Y and his colleagues and in the context of the corporate plan before such a key appointment (or key appointments) is/are made. An appointment now, before the concept of systematic human resources management had been firmly and widely established throughout the company, could be made only against woolly criteria.

The discussion groups were given limited objectives and they made the best use of limited time. What they could not do was look at the whole human resources area against some systematic framework.

The next step, using the framework that Y has developed, might be to read through the three *Reports* and record under each step what the organisation has already extensively said. The Study is only as good as the extent to which the knowledge in it is applied. There could hardly be a more purposeful way to apply it.

In the course of the discussions on the group-work, Y said, "I'm only as cynical as you make me." He was referring to the importance of assessment, to the need for it to be done properly, to the fact that at present it was not being done well. He said the first thing was to look at the present stock of managers. What better place to start? With, in parallel, clear signals from the chief executive about the kind of people needed for the future?

The chief executive spoke of the need for decisions followed by action: "Today's session means little until we have a plan that we have to live with." We need, he said, new skills to deliver on the new plan and new future.

He said, in effect, that he could judge only from their actions what people's basic beliefs were. "The basic belief is not there if we do nothing about it. It's only lip-service."

Two groups said they could not formulate a philosophy and the point was made, with which this adviser has some sympathy, that "our philosophy might be to do things". In other words, we don't fall into the trap of sequential thinking, waiting for one thing to be complete before attempting the next step — until finally we disappear up our own analyses.

The memorable point was made that the phrase "at the end of the day" should be expunged. There is no end to the day. The same applies to developing a human resources philosophy (or a mission statement). What is important is not so much the philosophy engraved on tablets of stone, but the continuing process of developing it: questioning it, understanding it, applying it and changing it as new insights come to hand. All of this makes for a flexible, creative, non-dependent organisation.

The adviser raised the question of the Fallacy of the Limited Good (and raised a few hackles when he said this was common in primitive tribes). This is the notion that you can have too much of a good thing, that the organisation could not contain a surfeit of bright people. This is almost like saying, "Keep the buggers ignorant or they'll get notions." The Fallacy of the Limited Good is the belief that the more power and information you give away, the more you lose power yourself. The opposite is the case. The more you empower your subordinates, the more you encourage them to influence you, the more you will influence them.

The prospect of bright but idle young managers floating aimlessly around is so inimical to the company's culture as hardly to be worth considering. If it were to happen, it would be evidence of a total absence of manpower planning.

In any event, the organisation must be replete with issues that need studying, forecasts that need to be made, projects that need advancing, things that could be meat and drink to young managers — and that line managers never have time to get around to.

Reference was made to the conflict between long-term and short-term, the perennial problem of the urgent driving out the important. In an imperfect world, there will always be some conflict. But if the urgent is consistently driving out the important, i.e. if the company is continually managed by expediency, then there is sure evidence of a vacuum of manpower policy.

Ansoff defined strategy as trying to ride a bicycle while you are assembling it. We do not know all we need to know about the contents of the company's human resources philosophy. But, following the Study and this conference, we certainly know enough to begin.

The traditional culture and skills of the company are powerful. There is now the realisation that, in addition (or, in company language, as an enhancement), the company needs also new beliefs and new skills to cope with a new future.

There is no doubt that they will come as circumstances force them. The challenge is to manage the change so that the company continues to get there first.

CHIEF EXECUTIVE'S CONCLUSIONS

The chief executive concluded:

- We may not have had formal written plans but there has always been an unwritten five-year plan.

- That plan happened.

- In 1985, when the first Study was conducted, nobody believed we would make the five-year target within four years.

- So something worked.

- If plans or targets go down on paper, I hope we have now taught all the doubting Thomases that they will happen.

- They will happen again — but this time out of a formal, detailed plan.

- We shall double in size by planning our way through. We shall try not to do it the hard way. We shall do it an easier way — by planning.

- The five-year plan is already there, in embryo, unwritten. In the next few months we shall get that two-pronged attack, finance and human resources, committed to paper — both at the same time.

- We have problems getting people to participate and people expect that getting the plan on paper will be the end of the exercise. That's far from the situation.

- The plan will hardly be on paper when the first year will have almost gone. There will be a constant updating on a rolling five-year basis.

- Getting participation is like pulling teeth out, slowly, one at a time.

- So far as human resources are concerned, I am concerned with the end, not the means. We do not yet have all the human resources tools or skills.

- We don't want eight or ten separate organisations recruiting against their own criteria and culture — and I living in another world wondering what the corporate culture is.

- It is Y who has to decide the kind of people we take into the organisation. The guidelines must be set by him: the numbers, the language skills, the technical capability, etc. This must come only from one office. The fine details can be decided at divisional level.

- At present we're doing a crash programme recruiting senior, experienced, marketing, R&D people and others. We had run into a brick wall and were forced to recruit senior people quickly. That showed the amount of planning we had done. Hopefully now, with manpower planning, we'll be able to see the brick wall from a distance instead of having to run into it first.

- Everybody has now accepted the corporate goals. Now we work them down through the divisions and then back up again.

- I am concerned about the fact that there may be a gap between myself and yourselves.

- How can we accept the mission statement and carry on as we've always been doing?

- How do we harness the wholehearted commitment of employees?

- It is strange that everybody apparently agrees with the mission statement yet does not seem to own it, to act on it.

- But the organisation, with all its warts, is still one of the best around. We may have done things more crudely than others. But you don't throw out the things that have worked for us. You enhance them.

- We must keep the organisation young. The organisation was young up to ten years ago. Then we all grew old together. The better the people you recruit, the better your own performance will be. Did we go out and recruit people less capable, less intelligent, people who did not form any threat? We recruited a poorer quality graduate.

- We are in division one in Ireland. Maybe we're not the best in division one. Maybe when we go to Europe we'll be in division four. It's easy to get to the top of the pile in Ireland. Yet it's important that, wherever we go, we carry with us our will to win.

- My last plea is to take things seriously (and not be thinking that we don't have to worry about that rubbish till we meet again).

- The Study was worthwhile. We broke down the mission statement. We have made a lot of progress.

ADVISER'S PRESENT (1998) COMMENTARY

The 1988/89 Study as it worked its way through was outlined in some detail because it illustrates the *sine qua non* for an effective Study: the commitment of the chief executive.

Participants in a Study know more about their company than I, an outsider, ever will, but they know about it from a particular angle, maybe from a narrow perspective. They have insights an outsider can seldom have. They are, however, unlikely to have the overview that can be obtained only by listening at length and in confidence to what their colleagues are saying. Like many forms of research, a Study is about bringing order out of what at first seems a chaos of views.

It is a search for order, for patterns, for interrelationships, for finding causes (which are not obvious) through studying effects (which are). It is not about imposing a preconceived or dogmatic order on things.

I was fond of saying in those days, "If a thing can't be written down, it doesn't exist." I still believe that but not so firmly as I did. One influence is that I have seen too many companies succeed splendidly with the sketchiest expressed strategies. That might be called the triumph of experience over intellect, thus calling down on my head the obloquy of academics.

Ten years ago, I probably had to rely more on what I read than on what I experienced. So I encouraged companies in which the participants perceived no strategy to bring orderliness into their affairs by adopting some form — any form — of systematic strategy formulation. It did not really matter which book or which management course they got it from, so long as it was consistent across the organisation and comprehensive — that is, nothing important left out. And done on a regular basis — that is, fixed dates on the calendar and tasks broken down and assigned.

I may have been influenced in this by my work over two years (1979–81) in Brussels with Igor Ansoff on the European Societal Strategy Project.[2] Ansoff's original discipline was mathematics. He is the most orderly and elegant of scholars. His major work, *Implementing Strategic Management*,[3] is probably the most comprehensive textbook there is on strategy. How many managers have studied it?

I had spent 21 years of my life in the Irish Management Institute, one of whose purposes was to make theory relevant to practice and vice versa. When I left, I wrote:

In this complex, hostile and changing scene, where the death rate and the birth rate of firms and products are accelerating, one cannot but have sympathy with the business manager who shows impatience at the world of ideas, of generalities.

I then quoted the famous passage from Keynes (1936):

> The idea of economists and political philosophers, both when they are right and when they are wrong, are more powerful than is commonly understood; indeed the world is ruled by little else. Practical men, who believe themselves to be quite exempt from any intellectual influences, are usually the slaves of some defunct economist. Madmen in authority, who hear voices in the air, are distilling their frenzy from some academic scribbler of a few years back. I am sure that the power of vested interests is vastly exaggerated compared with the gradual encroachment of ideas. Not, indeed, immediately, but after a certain interval; for in the field of economic and political philosophy there are not many who are influenced by new theories after they are 25 or 30 years of age, so that the ideas which civil servants and politicians and even agitators apply to current events are not likely to be the newest. But, soon or late, it is ideas, not vested interests, which are dangerous for good or evil.[4]

I went on:

> The environment in which practical businessmen operate is largely shaped by political action, action which gets its direction partly from a prevailing ideology or set of ideas. Businessmen have been apt to neglect this truth. Ideas do have legs. Businessmen cannot dismiss ideological debate as aca-

demic froth or idle intellectualising remote from the real world where things get done and wealth is created, because such debate has consequences which affect productive activity, however circuitous the route may sometimes seem.

The problem-solving perspective of the Irish manager is primarily a technological and economic one. He has little real exposure to the political, societal and cultural influences which affect business decisions. Within his perspective, he can be an incisive, convergent problem-solver. He can be quick to relate a problem to a precedent. He prefers the familiar solution to the novel one, an incremental change to a large one, a familiar risk to a gambler's plunge. He has only limited skills in solving novel problems which have no precedent.[5]

There is a whiff of arrogance there, of berating practising managers for not sharing my enthusiasm for the world of ideas. And, of course, leaving those managers totally unscathed. Gary Hamel wrote recently:

Strategists certainly can't be accused of being ignorant of the new competitive realities. But as informed as they may be, impactful they are not. Why? Because managers simply do not know what to do with all the wonderful concepts, frameworks and buzzwords that tumble from the papers of the *Harvard Business Review*, that join the aisles of bookstores, and that glisten in the slickly edited pages of business magazines.[6]

I still believe a systematic approach to strategy formulation is valuable but for reasons somewhat different to the ones I started out with. I would then have seen the principal outcome of a strategic process as a clear — i.e. expressed and understood — strategy. That is still important — knowing where you are going. But more important is the strategic process itself — provided it is: challenging (i.e. questioning unquestioned assumptions); rigorous (i.e. based on genuine information); collegial (i.e. open to new ideas and widely based); continuous (i.e. not giving up after one bad meeting). And strongly led, as the 1988/89 Study was by the chief executive. (It hardly needs saying that, if the process gets mixed up with the annual budget, all about numbers, it will die the death.) The more important outcome is the process's unifying force, the stimulation of creativity, the increase in mutual respect that comes from genuine collegiality, the focus on the future, on what business we are really in and on what must be done (rather than on present squabbles), leaving little time for cynicism or self-indulgence.

The remarks in my 1989 commentary about the Fallacy of the Limited Good were evidence of a growing conviction and designed to provoke (p. 173). I believe there is progress — at least in the (good) organisations that I have worked with. Increasingly, managers understand that the best way to influence their colleagues is to be influenced by them. This comes with self-confidence. A participant put it thus: "The CEO does not have to know when the last bus leaves for Hackball's Cross."

What is significant about this second Study of the same organisation is the increase in sophistication over three short years — and the corresponding increase in the sophistication of the Study. A Study must be responsive to the level of sophistication in a company. If it lagged behind it would be discredited. If it were too far ahead, it would become irrelevant — theoretical in the pejorative sense.

Notes

1. Dorothy Leonard-Barton (1995), *Wellsprings of Knowledge: Building and Sustaining the Sources of Innovation*, Boston: Harvard Business School Press, p. xv. See also: Kenichi Ohmae (1990), *The Borderless World: Power and Strategy in the Interlinked Economy*, London: Collins, p. 193: "It is hard to let old beliefs go . . . like a man who has worn eyeglasses so long that he forgets he has them on, we forget that the world looks to us the way it does because we have become used to seeing it that way through a particular set of lenses. Today, however, we need new lenses. And we need to throw the old ones away."

2. European Institute for Advanced Studies in Management, European Foundation for Management Development (1981), *Facing Realities, The Report of the European Societal Strategy Project*, Brussels.

3. Igor Ansoff (1984), *Implementing Strategic Management*, Englewood Cliffs, NJ: Prentice Hall.

4. John Maynard Keynes (1936), *The General Theory of Employment, Interest and Money*, 1965 reprint, Harcourt Brace and Co.

5. Ivor Kenny (1984), *Government and Enterprise in Ireland*, Dublin: Gill and Macmillan, pp. 77 *et seq.*

6. Gary Hamel (1998), "Strategy Innovation and the Question for Value", *Sloan Management Review*, Winter, p. 9.

Chapter 8

STUDY 5 (1990/91):
TIME TO IMPLEMENT

INTRODUCTION

Study 5 was the second of three State companies in this book. It was mainly in the commodity business but with some added-value branded products. It had come successfully through a period of substantial change led by a charismatic chief executive. There was now a desire to settle down.

It is all very well for outsiders (like myself) who carry no personal responsibility for an enterprise to preach the need for continuous change and questioning. Organisations also need periods of stability — if only to catch their breath and to understand fully where they have arrived. And that period of stability (as we noted with Study 2) is the best time to intervene in a company.

There were 44 participants in the Study.

THE ISSUES: PARTICIPANTS' VIEWS IN THE INTERIM (DIAGNOSTIC) REPORT

Against the background of substantial recent achievements and change, there is evidence of *uncertainty* — where do we go now? — with consequent lowering of morale.

Comments on *strategy* follow on from the feeling of uncertainty. They show some confusion, some lack of faith in the organisation's strategic ability and in the quality of the information on which strategic decisions are based.

The focus of the Study is the organisation as a whole, but *strategic options* are worked out in practice in the separate divisions. In line with the uncertainty, views on strategic options for the divisions are diffuse: there is no coherent pattern.

Nonetheless, there is faith in the organisation, in its *opportunities*, and in the inherent value of its business. This is balanced by some pessimistic views about the future and its *constraints*.

There are varying views about the company's historical social (State) objective of maintaining *employment*.

While there is support for the concept of new businesses, the principal question raised was about the company's seriousness in the matter, about whether it is really prepared to back new ventures. It is noted that no venture of significant size is contemplated and there is an appreciation that any new venture would take a long time — five years — to pay back. It is felt that there are no clear criteria for new businesses and some questioning of the company's capability to manage them: did it have the necessary skills, environment, systems, structures and leadership?

What is needed is a period of *consolidation*, of doing well what the company is doing, of avoiding "mega-solutions".

There is a recognition that a consolidation phase might require skills different from those with which the first change phase was managed.

There is the acknowledgement that the organisation has gone through a profound change and some realisation that change would now be continuous, despite the desire for a period of consolidation.

Change in an organisation is always uneven: it moves at different paces, it is welcomed by some and questioned or resented by others.

The uncertainty running through the above views is reinforced by what is widely perceived as a gap between thought and action, rhetoric and reality. There is a growing impatience with reports, task forces and consultants and an expressed need for decision and action.

The gap between rhetoric and reality is felt most acutely by line management, who feel they lose credibility with their workforce. As one participant put it: "If people can't believe what I tell them, I'm lost."

REMEDY: PARTICIPANTS' VIEWS IN THE *SECOND* (*PLANNING*) *REPORT*

Uncertainty, caused by lack of a clear, shared strategy, was a primary issue in the *Diagnostic Report*.

Even though the second phase of the Study was conducted at the same time as a five-year plan was being prepared, uncertainty was undiminished. Comments about lack of strategy had a sharper edge, some now querying the *raison d'être* of the company. There was an expressed need for clearer signals from the top.

Consolidation was seen in the *Interim Report* as the first necessary step in reducing uncertainty. This was reinforced in this *Report*, with some greater clarity about what consolidation actually meant. There was also an emerging belief that consolidation by itself would not be sufficient, that further radical change would be needed.

There were mixed, generally critical, views about the *strategic process*. The organisation was seen to devote more energy to process — the *how* — than to the business and the customer — the *what*. The point was made that overall strategy was not just the sum of divisional strategies.

There was a clear consensus in the *Interim Report* that commercialisation — proximity to the customer, concern for quality, profit maximisation — was the way to go, but the company's managers were not businessmen.

The view that the commercial route was the way to go was now unequivocal.

One of the reasons for this was that the company was a State body and "the whole state system is the very opposite of commerciality".

There was the view that you cannot have commerciality without ownership, that divisions cannot behave commercially without autonomy — freedom from both state and corporate constraints.

The private entrepreneur's attitude to money was contrasted with the company's.

The point was made that commercialism's first concern was the customer.

ADVISER'S COMMENTARY (1991)

(When the Study was completed, I wrote the following, probably from an anxiety that nothing much was going to happen.)

The best way to get a perspective on the 1991 Study is to go back and read right through the *Diagnostic Report*, particularly the chapter on strategy.

There was then a pervasive feeling of uncertainty about the future of the company. There was confusion about strategy and no coherent pattern in the views on strategic options. There were varying views about the company's historical objective of maintaining employment.

Moving on five months to the *Final Report*, uncertainty was undiminished. This was curious, as the second phase of the Study was conducted at the same time as a five-year plan was prepared. However, in that sec-

ond phase, views on strategy had a sharper focus and
came right down to the *raison d'être* of the company —
where, perhaps, wisdom begins.

A "commercial scenario" emerged in the second
phase. There was some tendency to look it squarely in
the face, turn around and walk in the opposite direction.

The final conferences were unequivocal — and for
"unequivocal", it is reasonable to read "an end to uncertainty". The nettle was grasped — at least intellectually. There was agreement that, if the company did not
continue to serve the changing needs of its customers
profitably, it could exist only in an atmosphere of failure, blame and handouts.

One of the barriers to commerciality was "We are
not businessmen", a fact of life over which there was
some hand-wringing. There is only one way the company's managers will be businessmen and that is to
manage under commercial constraints — i.e., with their
jobs depending on the bottom line, with no state-
sponsored refuge where someone will take care of them
if they do not return a profit.

It emerged in the latter stages of the Study that
many, if not most, of the barriers to the company's development were internal-and-now, not external and
"inherited". In any event, management's job is to identify those areas that are within its discretion, and to exploit and widen them constantly; and, conversely, to
spend little time in contemplation of those areas it can-

not influence. In Hermann Kahn's words, "If at first you don't succeed, give up."

The company's managers might well retort, "It's not that simple", and of course it isn't. It was seen clearly at the concluding conferences that the company is a State body with the special constraints that brings. State-sponsored chief executives spend a lot more time managing upwards to the shareholder than their counterparts in the private sector do.

The chief executive in any organisation is at the pivotal point, the centre of the X. It is the point at which all the complexities of an organisation come together. It is the point at which all the stakeholders with their competing needs and aspirations meet. And yet it is the point from which clear statements of direction are expected.

I said in the *Final Report*:

> A strong visible and energetic leader may spur different psychological responses. Some individuals may become overly dependent on the leader and in some cases whole organisations become dependent. Everyone else stops initiating actions and waits for the leader to provide directions; individuals may become passive or reactive. At the other extreme, others may be uncomfortable with a strong personal presence and spend time and energy demonstrating how the leader is wrong. In the presence of a strong leader, people may become hesitant to disagree or come into conflict with the leader.

Both these phenomena were evident in the Study. It would be strange if they were not. The company has come through a classic charismatic leadership phase and has not yet made the necessary adjustment to the instrumental leadership phase. I said:

> Effective re-orientations seem to be characterised by the presence of another type of leadership behaviour which focuses not on the excitement of individuals and changing their goals, needs or aspirations, but on making sure that individuals in the senior team and throughout the organisation behave in ways needed for change to occur.

Whether it is called "instrumental leadership" or "mundane management" or "consolidation" or whatever, a clear message from the Study is that the company's managers want to get on with it. They have had enough of task forces and consultants and reports, of process — the How. They want to tackle the What.

There are now — at least to this observer — sufficiently clear, shared strategic guidelines within which the three main divisions can find their own commercial destiny, while a slimmed-down head office continues to manage the relationship with the shareholder and becomes a support service.

Support from head office is critical. For many managers, truly commercial criteria will be taking them into uncharted waters. It would be unreasonable to expect them all instantly to swim. Some may sink. This is where a helping hand and a kindly ear will reap rewards rich in loyalty and commitment — and where macho management will fail. Macho management is more often than not the outward expression of a manager's inward uncertainty.

There is an opportunity here for the company's managers to maintain their essential decency while beating the hell out of the competition.

I am still puzzled about why the first one of the two final conferences seemed at the time to go badly and the second one well. We had a better timetable and stricter guidelines for the second one — but it could not have been only that. Following the first conference, a senior manager telephoned me. I shared his disappointment except when he said, "There was nothing new." There is indeed nothing new in the sense of a new vision or a new strategy. As Mintzberg wrote:

> Organisations that reassess their strategies continuously are like individuals who reassess their jobs or their marriages continuously — in both cases, people will drive themselves crazy or else reduce themselves to inaction. So-called strategic planning must be recognised for what it is: a means not to create strategy, but to programme a strategy already created — to work out its implications formally.[1]

I would be very disappointed if, following the full frontal of the Study, there was anything new in the sense of something emerging that we did not already know about. The Study was comprehensive.

It must be remembered that as recently as the spring of this year (1991), an organisation blockage survey was conducted. It showed that the most significant blockage was unclear aims.

The quest for clarity is never-ending. The job of management is by definition open-ended. You can never go home on Friday serene in the belief that all is ready for Monday. It is always "one damn thing after another".

To look for any clarity greater than is evident from the *Reports* is to search for the Holy Grail. It would be to fall back into the dreary trap of circular discussions on process.

We can never know all we want to know. (Lord Acton never wrote a complete book because he was constantly searching for perfection. When he died they found a cellar full of exquisite scholarly notes.) Since strategy is an imperfect process we shall learn more by trying to implement it than we shall by reflecting on it.

The company has achieved much. It now needs to build a commercial track record. That means its divisions may teeter on the brink of going out of business — that is the commercial condition. That is the essence of commerciality. And it means divisional managers accepting personal responsibility for that fact.

But commerciality means more. It means an obsession with the customer. The reports at the conferences are fresh, creative, thoughtful and informed. If they have a weakness it is that there is little talk about the customer. In the introduction to the *Final Report*, it was said that sovereignty was moving slowly, but inexorably, to the customer.

Maybe that criticism is somewhat harsh, because many of the things that need to be done are ultimately directed towards the customer: quality, delivery, price and bloody-minded efficiency intolerant of excuses.

There are many messages in the Study. It will repay rereading. (It would be a dreadful waste if it were to suffer death in the drawer.) If there is one message above any other, it is to get on with the job.

ADVISER'S PRESENT (1998) COMMENTARY

I have nothing to add to that. Nor would I change it. It is evidence of a growing conviction: "Since strategy is an imperfect process we shall learn more by trying to implement it than we shall by reflecting on it."

There was more than an echo here of what we met with in another state company, Study 2 in 1986: the desire of executives to be "businessmen", focused on the customer.[2]

From three State companies covered in this book, and from other Studies, there is no doubt that State companies have a softer, less driven culture than private enterprise. They are also subject to the unique frustrations outlined in the *Introduction*.

In practically all other Studies, the emphasis was on introducing some form of systematic strategy-making where there was a vacuum. In this instance, things were reversed. The emphasis was on getting on with the job and with less debate about who we were and where we were going.

Russell Ackoff wrote:

> A good deal of the corporate planning I have ob-
> served is like a ritual rain dance; it has no effect on
> the weather that follows, but those engaged in it
> think it does. Moreover, it seems to me that much
> of the advice and instruction related to corporate
> planning is directed at improving the dancing, not
> the weather.[3]

Notes

1. Henry Mintzberg (1987), "Crafting Strategy", *Harvard Business Review*, July/August, p. 73.

2. This is what G.P. Dempsey of Aer Lingus, the Irish State-owned airline, said: "Enterprise and innovative leadership have flour- ished in our state-owned companies. Over the years many have out-performed the private sector in this respect. However, even though the dictionary may show me wrong, I make a distinc- tion between being enterprising and being entrepreneurial. I believe that an entrepreneur is essentially one who owns or controls a business and thus drives unrelentingly for profit, both for reward and assurance of continuity. Thus both private ownership and profit come into the picture. This does not sit well in a state-owned company, partly because of ideology and partly because the state companies are usually service or utility suppliers and, up to recent years at any rate, were not wholly committed to profit." Ivor Kenny (1991), *Out on Their Own*, Dublin: Gill and Macmillan, p. 72.

3. Russell L. Ackoff (1981), *Creating the Corporate Future*, London: Wiley, p. ix.

Chapter 9

STUDY 6 (1992/93): THE STATE IN BUSINESS

INTRODUCTION

Study 6 was in many ways the opposite of Study 5. Another State company, it felt it had mastered its essentially local mandate and wanted to broaden into (more exciting) international activities.

When Sir Edmund Hillary was asked why he wanted to climb Mount Everest, he replied, "Because it is there." Fine for a heroic mountaineer. Hardly sufficient as a business objective.

The most powerful question advisers can ask is "Why?" But they must be sure they get the answer. As Michael Porter put it:

> Increased attention to formal strategic planning has highlighted questions that have long been of concern to managers . . . Yet most of the emphasis in formal strategic planning processes has been on asking those questions in an organised and disciplined way rather than on answering them.[1]

Advisers must keep asking why, peeling away the layers, until they come to the real reason why people and

organisations do certain things. "Because it is there" is
not a sufficient reason. Neither is excitement. Excitement, challenge, may be the spark that lights the fire so
that a strategy "emerges". And the strategy that does
emerge may well carry the organisation through. I am
not suggesting, to change the metaphor, that we continually pull the plant up to examine the roots. But I
have found it useful to ask "Why are we doing this?" or
"Why are we continuing to do this?" And I have occasionally found the answers objectively suspect.

There is an Irish saying: *There's a reason for everything. And then there's the real reason.*

The chief executive's summing up of this Study is a
classic of its kind and is given *in extenso* below.

There were 49 participants.

THE ISSUES: SUMMARY OF PARTICIPANTS' VIEWS IN THE *SECOND REPORT*

Strategy

The chapter on strategy, dealing with a complex subject, begins with some questions, particularly about
growth and profitability.

There is concern that the overall strategy of the
company is unclear.

There are criticisms of the strategic process, though
some participants see it improving. There is the view
that it is top-down, not widely shared, that Business
Units put in their particular bits in the absence of a
common vision, that it is primarily opportunistic.

At least part of the motivation for getting into overseas activities is seen as the excitement, the glamour,
the sense of achievement, contrasted in a few views
with the perceived banality of the core business. There
is consensus that this particular move was opportunistic as opposed to strategic.

The general views on international strategy are unclear and show a level of uncertainty but with a perceived need to move from opportunism to longer-term
profitability.

Overseas work is seen as providing learning opportunities but people are not being trained specifically
for it. Overseas development in terms of both manpower and preoccupation are seen as constituting some
danger to core domestic activities.

Privatisation

Privatisation as an issue did not merit a separate chapter in the *Interim Report*. The summary in that *Report*
was: insofar as views on privatisation were expressed,
the majority felt that, while there might be some difficulties in the way, privatisation was coming. There was
some concern that the company would lose its public
service ethos, but the majority of those who expressed
views were in favour of privatisation.

As the Study progressed, privatisation moved up the
scale.

The company was on a growth path and the only
way it could grow and have access to funds was
through privatisation.

However, questions were asked: Do we really want privatisation? If so, could we decide now? Have we thought of the consequences for our jobs? *Cui bono?*

It was felt that privatisation must be driven by the centre. It would be refreshing to make clear management's interest in privatisation — freedom, energy.

It was felt that the depth of cultural change, in privatisation and beyond, should not be underestimated.

CHIEF EXECUTIVE'S VERBATIM REMARKS AT CONCLUDING CONFERENCES

The chief executive told the concluding conferences:

One of our great needs is to operate more commercially, to have greater measures of performance and to focus on doing things because they are commercially the right things to do, rather than having other reasons for doing them.

Your view about privatisation is that it's not urgent, not the number one priority for us. One of the points that Ivor made is that it's important to see privatisation as a means rather than an end and this is something that becomes more and more clear to me as I look at it. We can't just take a simple-minded view that privatisation is good and we're going to go for it. You have to have some compelling argument for it, real reasons. We have done nothing at all yet to demonstrate that we need privatisation. It's just an opinion that floats around. Privatisation is not a goal. It means that you have plans to do certain things and you say that privatisation is the only way to do those things. We're talking about privatisation before we have the plans. I never said I wasn't in favour of privatisation. I'm just saying we have never established the need for it in any compelling way. Given the barriers to it that I see politically, we have to establish the need for it before we can go for it.

On the strategic process: after discussion with the senior management group over a long period, I became frustrated because we couldn't seem to agree anything very precisely and I went off and, based on a whole lot of things that had been said, I wrote the strategy and I presented it to the senior management group. The senior management group said they agreed, there were a few inputs and changes made. I then went to the Board with it and they all said yes and then I came back and went round the different areas and I presented it to the management groups and everybody said yes — and then people said later that they didn't agree with the strategy at all.

Maybe some people are not serious about the strategic plan but I don't think it's true that everybody lies all the time about everything. I think there would be some dishonesty and some fear of speaking up and taking a position about things. I'm not sure to what extent people have to sign on and agree totally with the overall plan. If what an individual Business Unit is doing is defined within an overall plan and if they do it and are happy to do it, then it doesn't matter if they actually agree with all the other constituents of that plan.

The interesting element in this is that it touches on a few things that became very controversial and became the centrepiece of some of the presentations we had earlier in the week. One is this question of everybody signing on and no going back. We talked about mavericks, people doing their own thing, people who agree something and pull out of it. There was a very strong view from everybody around the room that this can't be allowed, that I shouldn't be as tolerant of mavericks as I am and that I shouldn't allow people to do their own thing.

If the implication is that everybody should be involved in every aspect of the strategic plan, then I have to say I disagree with it. One of the points that has been made fairly strongly to me is that this so-called divisiveness arises from our trying to make people agree to things that they don't have to agree to. If you're in a particular unit doing a particular job, you don't have to agree with somebody else in another unit who is doing something remote from you. It doesn't matter to him. The broad strategy needs to be agreed, the long-term picture, but the process you go through in arriving at specifics doesn't require everybody to agree. People have criticised the Thursday morning meetings, seeing them as myself and a few corporate people sitting there who are interested in all these things but the individuals from the Business Units are sitting there listening to reports about things they couldn't care less about. The agenda is useful to me and for some corporate people but at the expense of huge hostility from some of the people in the Business Units who have to endure it.

There is a feeling that the larger executive group needs to meet together at least once a year for real work, such as the annual review of the strategic plan.

Some people have asked what is the role of the senior executive group — if people won't talk about each other's areas and won't get involved or won't criticise someone else's plans. I think it's something that the senior executive group has to address. What kind of environment do they want to work in? Is it one where important issues about each other's areas can be discussed and thrashed out and everybody can have a reasonable input into it? That could make the Thursday meetings much longer. It could make them much more interesting in some ways, because instead of just sitting there listening to reports all the time, you were actually expected to contribute. It would be a change of culture. I think I'll have to talk to the senior group about that, whether they want to do those kind of things or whether occasionally we should have a session where we talk about a particular unit in depth.

A lot of what I have got from the last two days is new and food for thought. I was very pleased with the level of frankness. I'm told some people are afraid of me. I don't know what I can do to stop that. I'm just trying to do the job of chief executive the best way I can. I value it when people speak out. I've got a few messages personally. For example, that I shouldn't let people get away with things, as this can be seen as unfair. On the wider things about the company I have had a whole lot of things reinforced. The need for us to professionalise and to clear up any messiness is very acutely felt. I'm willing to tolerate a *bit* of messiness in the interest of getting energy released. The more you put people into very rigid little boxes, the less energy you get. There is a very clear need for mobility and I need to move on that. I'm glad that you yourselves are recognising that it is a disability in the organisation that people tend to stay in the same place for too long. We owe it to each other to address that.

I plan to hold a one-off conference where I'll come back to you and say what I'm going to do. That will be in about 6/8 weeks from now.

It's the end of four days for me of very interesting exchanges and hearing a whole lot of things for the first time and hearing a whole lot of angles on things that are very helpful and refreshing. What we've been trying to do for some months now is to find out what the barriers are. When I read the *Reports* I was shocked sometimes at how much ignorance there was. Some people made very strong statements that simply weren't true, they didn't match the facts. In the second *Report* we seemed to be even further apart. But to my great pleasure I found this week has been very much a constructive exercise. There is a huge amount of territory that's shared, as well as the things that cause the problems. It's great that everybody thinks we should grow profitably both at home and abroad and that we can. There is no hint of defeatism from anybody; it's been about how do you get it going. I think we have done something this week that's going to be of huge importance to us. You've left me with a lot of conflicting suggestions, requests and solutions and I'll have to comb through those and come back to you about them.

While Ivor would say we're not very commercial, I would say that for a State company we're very commercial and that's an advantage.

I have a lot to think about and a lot to work on. I have a great belief in the possibilities for us. We have an awful lot going for us, unique things. If we can put the right thoughts together, the right ideas and the right structures together, I know the enthusiasm is there and we can really direct it very well.

I know I am putting my neck on the block now but I would feel that the things I will do now as a result of all I have heard from the managers in the company this week will be good things. I think they will make things better. I know they will.

ADVISER'S PRESENT (1998) COMMENTARY

The chief executive was firmly in control of the concluding conferences, yet open and honest about, for example, his struggle with a strategic process.

I distrust group-work. It can be good for getting genuine consensus. It can be deceptive in getting apparent consensus, particularly if the process is chaired by a chief executive. Few managers are determined enough to pursue an argument if they get slapped down by a CEO. Weaker ones may rally to his cause to curry favour. Many will sit back and watch the bull-fight, amused or bored.

I have hardly conducted a Study where anybody was satisfied with the quality of meetings. It would be helpful if at each meeting someone was deputed by the chairperson to summarise the output of the meeting before it breaks up: in effect writing instant minutes (what has been decided, who is going to do what and by when, how will it be reported back); together with a commentary on the process (was time spent in repetitive argument or point-scoring); was the meeting dominated by the chairperson or other member; was everybody given a fair hearing or were people squashed; did the chairperson summarise accurately the gist of the meeting? . . . And so on. This is such basic stuff that I am almost ashamed to write it. Yet how often does it get done? More time must be wasted at futile and dreary meetings than at most other human activities.[2]

The concluding conferences for the Studies work well, almost without exception (see Study 5, p. 193). The reason is (a) the extensive preparation and (b) the unequivocal focus. Perhaps there is a lesson there.

Lack of preparation for a meeting is the unforgivable sin. A State company chief executive (not a company studied here) told me a member of his board would ostentatiously slit open the envelope containing his board pack as he sat down at the boardroom table.

The clarity about privatisation being a means not an end was useful. The objective reasons for privatisation are freedom to manoeuvre and grow and access to capital.[3] The motivation is often at a more basic level: high salaries and escape from the suffocating grip of the civil service and the politicians. The chief executive in this Study, a man of strong integrity, was unmoved by the prospect of a high salary and was skilled at navigating his way through the bureaucracy.

Notes

1. Michael E. Porter (1980), *Competitive Strategy: Techniques for Analysing Industries and Competitors*, New York: Free Press, pp. xiii–xiv.

2. "To work well, boards need both freedom and order. It is the chairman's job to ride both tigers. One thing that does not seem to work well is to consider at the same meeting both long- and short-term issues. The urgent always drives out the important. A solution is to consider them at different times and places. *Decision-making meetings* can be held around the boardroom table with an eye on the clock. Twice-yearly *strategy-making* is away from the office in a comfortable country house, with a minimum of formality, a lot of time and talk — but with the chairman keeping an eagle eye on the process, constantly summarising, preferably on a flip-chart, so that there is a feeling of progress, of momentum, and a minimum of repetition and wheelspin. Perhaps once a year the workings of the board itself might be put on the agenda because the best boards can develop bad habits and blind spots. An outside observer is useful here." Ivor Kenny (1994), *Boardroom Practice*, Second Edition, Dublin: UCD, pp. 49–51.

3. "The broad-reaching change and the large number of interested parties involved in privatisation makes such programs prone to carry many levels of 'intellectual baggage'. Among others, the following objectives are mentioned frequently in connection with privatisation:
   • Reduce the government's operating deficit.
   • Raise cash through SOE sales.
   • Generate new sources of tax revenue.

- Reduce external debt, largely through debt equity swaps.
- Deepen domestic capital markets and broaden domestic equity ownership.
- 'Democratization of capital'.
- Encourage the return of flight capital.
- Promote domestic investment.
- Attract direct foreign investment and new technology.
- Increase domestic and international business confidence.
- Increase competition.
- Create opportunities for employment through real growth.
- Increase productive and operating efficiency.
- 'Turn around' or restructure sick SOEs.
- Increase exports.
- Improve the quality of services, and
- Reduce the role of the state in the economy.

A number of these objectives, such as reducing the government's deficit, raising cash from the sale of SOEs or reducing external debt, are potentially direct and immediate outcomes of privatisation. Other objectives, such as increasing productive efficiency, absorption of new technology, and creating employment opportunities through growth are longer-term objectives and depend on what the private sector brings to the table."

For Lieberman, however, the multitude of objectives essentially combine into three key issues:

"1. *Get government out of business to the fullest extent possible* so as to strengthen private market forces and competition in order to increase productivity, efficiency, quality and service in the provision of goods and services to the population.

2. *Generate new sources of cash flow and financing for enterprise*, such as increased domestic investment, return of flight capital, direct foreign investment, external lending and deepening of domestic capital markets.

3. Reduce the government's fiscal deficit and its external and internal debt."

Ira W. Lieberman (1993), "Privatisation: an Overview", *The Columbia Journal of World Business*, Spring, pp. 11–12.

See also Introduction.

Chapter 10

STUDY 7 (1996/97):
WHERE SHOULD STRATEGY BEGIN?

INTRODUCTION

Study 7 was a very large company, part of an international group mainly in the commodity but also in the value-added business.

The chief executive asked one of his senior colleagues to analyse the report of the final conference. He came up with about 60 recommendations: some on detail, some on fundamentals. At the review conference it was reported that practically all of them had been implemented.

There were 56 participants.

ISSUES: SUMMARY OF THE PARTICIPANTS' VIEWS IN THE *INTERIM REPORT*

There was consensus that there was no *clear* strategy — or even *no* strategy for the company. The point was made that the company had made mistakes and that future mistakes, because of the company's size, could be big ones.

There was consensus that there was no *strategic guidance* from the centre. The vacuum was filled by individual companies formulating their individual strategies.

There were several *strategic actions* suggested, with some threads of consensus running through them.

There was consensus that there was no *strategic process*. There was consensus that a strategic process must be top-down *and* bottom-up and must focus on the *business* of the company, not merely on numbers.

ADVISER'S FIRST COMMENTARY (1997)

At what point does strategy at country or plant level give way to strategy at HQ level? Underlying this debate is a more fundamental question about what distinguishes a group from the relatively standalone businesses of which it is made up. What should be the distinguishing features of strategy at HQ level?

The distinction between group and business-unit strategy can be expressed as shown in the table on the following page. It is taken from Hay and Williamson's excellent *Strategy Handbook*:[1]

> A summary runs the risk of implying that, between group and business-unit strategy, there is a hard and fast distinction. There is not.

> Although strategy at these two levels is concerned with separate sets of issues, the boundary is often blurred. Overlaps occur, group corporate influence has a profound effect upon the strategy of an individual business and, indeed, the business itself is,

in a sense, the vehicle through which group corporate strategy is realised. Decisions made at the centre, such as those relating to acquisition or divestment, are *de facto* decisions about the positioning of a business in relation to the product market and competitors within that market. Therefore, rather than accentuating the distinction, the most fruitful way of viewing these two dimensions of strategy, about which there is often much confusion, is to see them as being part of a seamless web: a web in which the strategy that is pursued at different levels throughout the company is coherent and consistent.

Country/Company Strategy	*HQ Corporate Strategy*
Competing for	Competing for
• Products	• Finance
• Customers	• Management
• Suppliers	• Companies
Managing	Managing
• Activities	• Process
	• Interrelationships
Via intervention	Via reinforcement
Creating value by	Creating value by
• Business-to-market fit	• Business-to-portfolio fit

REMEDY: SUMMARY OF PARTICIPANTS' VIEWS IN THE *PLANNING REPORT*

In the *Interim Report*, there was consensus: that there was no *clear* strategy — or even *no* strategy for the company; that there was no *strategic guidance* from the centre; and that the vacuum was filled by individual companies formulating their individual strategies.

In this *Report*, there is, on the part of some participants, a modification of that view, a belief or assumption that *there is a strategy at the overall level*, imperfectly communicated. There is no modification of the view that there is *no clear strategy at this company's HQ level*, that that is where there is a strategic vacuum.

Evidence of that strategic vacuum is the number of *unanswered strategic questions*. On *specific strategies* — the agenda for future actions beyond this Study — there is a sharpening of the perspective since the *Interim Report*.

In this *Report*, while still agreeing that the process must be top-down and bottom-up, there is agreement also that *leadership* of the process must come from the top, which should articulate both the vision for the Group as a whole and the strategic framework within which the company would plan. The instrument for making strategy happen is seen as a *strategic group* or *executive committee*.

There followed a rich harvest of views giving many of the elements of a strategic process and of its content. Some of them are given verbatim below:

"Strategy and the strategic process are the number one issue."

"No process = no strategy."

"We should not be predicting the future, we should be making it."

"*Now* is the time to build the strategy. Now is also the time to face any mistakes we've made because of lack of strategy in the past."

"We have built the organisation. Now we need to empower the people in it and plant the seeds for the future."

"In some shape or form the Group should put the company in its general strategic context once a year so that everybody knows where they stand."

"There *is* no clear strategy. We need a strategy formulated by the leaders. We need a strategy of leadership, not of blindly following. We first need a strong, comprehensive vision of the future. An incomplete strategy is a bad strategy. We need to apply the rules of war. We may need to lose battles to win the war."

"Strategy formulation requires first an accurate analysis of the customer, the product and the competition. We need to understand the trends and the fact that they can be modified. And it requires a lot of teamwork. The strategy should be clear to us but not to the competition. This depends entirely on the motivation of the manager − people who live for their work, even before money. And the crucial point is that there is no process."

"We need to see ourselves in a broad Group strategy. In the 'how' of how we'll get there, the cultural issues will become clear. This is a job for the top people."

"There's no mission statement that gets to people's hearts. We need a clear, shared goal/mission statement. We're doing it in my company: good customer relations through good quality product; cost reduction/efficiency; motivating people. We ask people to make their budget around these three key issues."

"I would modify my early remarks about strategy being both top-down and bottom-up. I now believe it must be top-down but after considering and testing all the bottom-up strategies."

"You can't have a strategy decided by a committee. You pool the ideas, test the water, then the decision is taken by a very small committee and finally decided by the CEO. We're in a state where we have lots of meetings — strategic decision-making is about *decision*-making. We need to be very careful that we don't end up with a lowest common denominator strategy."

"We need a strategy that is the best for the long-term future even if everybody does not agree with it. Then you *implement* that strategy even if it causes some people to leave because they cannot support it. And we must understand that strategy is a living thing subject to continuous adjustment. What we have now is a thick book of numbers that nobody takes the slightest notice of. Following strategy we need a clear consistent structure."

"Who should write the strategy — at each level? The boss sets the direction, then encourages participation, then sets his seal on the strategy. Then he is responsible for participating at a higher level. Then any changes or modifications are communicated down. It's a continuous process."

"We need a clear statement about what businesses we are in and what we are not in."

"Structure precedes strategy. Then strategy dictates structure. It's an iterative, circular, continuous process."

"Our 'strategy' is formulated in a vacuum of self-complacency. The top people spend their time fire-fighting. There is no time for brainstorms, for constructive thinking. Strategy should be a qualitative rather than quantitative exercise. Profit is important but the future is more important."

"To have a strategy, you need comprehensive measures, not just historical budgets."

"We need more discretion from the centre, to get a *combined* strategy. To get that you need to have a team that understands all the activities and that is supplied with very good information on the markets."

"The best way to have a successful strategy is to invest in a continuous feedback, to make sure that people understand what the CEO says. It's not enough to make a speech and to be applauded."

"To have a clear strategy is not enough. And everyone may not agree entirely with it. But absolutely they have to *understand* the strategy."

"We should look into the future a little more. We should think in terms of long-term actions. We should devote more *time* and resources to this. The actions are: to look for innovation; new technologies; and to train our managers for future respon-

sibility. We have to put new blood in the system —
an action today for a result tomorrow. It is good
we're investing in best practice, low cost production, but we need more innovation for tomorrow.
This is a change in style."

"This was the most interesting chapter of the entire
study. A clear vision of the future makes the management more comfortable. We have to dedicate
time and resources to *where* we want to go, *how*
and *what we want to become* in five years' time.
That's a good target. I am sure the top people have
definite plans but they have never been communicated. Once defined, the plans must be communicated down."

"Strategy can't just be developed by senior management. Even junior managers must participate in
the process."

"We should have *real* strategic conferences: genuine working parties looking at the future, asking
what 'best' means."

"When you ask someone for a strategy, you get
thousands of figures. We have to *train* people to
build strategies — and that goes for the very top.
Here we need help."

"Strategy should be one of our priorities in training."

"A former chairman of a multinational company
said, 'Your strategic will is to be present at the year
2000 dinner, but first you will be present at break-
fast tomorrow.' So my first job is to take care of the
medium- and short-term strategy. It's not possible

to give to 100 people the long-term strategy because it's top-secret."

"The nub of the study is the vacuum of strategy.
But before that comes a regular strategic process
that addresses *all* the problems, e.g. the role (if
any) of HQ, the financial issues, the HR issues —
all this against the background of clear objectives."

CHIEF EXECUTIVE'S SUMMING UP AT THE CONCLUDING CONFERENCES

My last word is an absolute commitment that I will respond to the report on this conference within four to six
weeks of receiving it. I will respond to each member of
this conference and tomorrow's conference with decisions we're prepared to confirm within four to six
weeks. I'll be calling upon individual people to help
carry some of the decisions forward. We don't want to
hang about. I don't want to be discussing this in two
years' time. I want to see action programmes and decisions implemented very fast after our confirmation of
the action programme. You'll all have to help in some
way or another to see this forward.

ADVISER'S SECOND COMMENTARY (1997)

I believe you are at Point A on Charles Handy's
S-Curve.[2] You are certainly still in the ascendant, not in
the descendant. You are a very successful company.
Studies like this work only in successful companies.
Hopefully now we have many of the ingredients of fu-
ture success.

If we continue to involve the organisation widely in the gathering of information and ideas, in identifying the internal blockages, as we did in the Studies; if we separate out the strategic process and put in place a proper information-gathering resource, skill and system, then we shall have the beginnings of a strategic process with the sole purpose of strengthening the company's competitive advantage.

ADVISER'S PRESENT (1998) COMMENTARY

Following on this Study, a company-wide strategic process was established with the help of a distinguished consultant who, incidentally, was privy to the Study *Reports* and with whom I had a lengthy and productive hand-over meeting.

The Study led to significant changes in personnel, in structure and in process. At the review meeting nine months later, as we were breaking up, a senior manager asked for the microphone and said simply, "I think I speak for us all when I say things are much better." The Study led to two further Studies within the same Group, too identifiable to be included here. (One is very shortly summarised in Chapter 11.)

To reinforce something I have already said: the key ingredient in the success of the Study was the relationship of total trust between the chief executive and myself. He was a tough guy, professional, willing to listen, impatient for change. Unusually, structural changes were made in the course of the two further Studies, both of which he commissioned, but only after he had received the *Interim Diagnostic Report*. He made the changes in the sure knowledge that he had consensus for them. When they were implemented it was done with minimum disturbance and maximum support.

As I write, the new widely based strategic process is addressing fundamental strategic issues. The first major strategic conference following a year's work by product groups was held in July 1998. The process is working well.

Notes

1. Michael Hay and Peter Williamson (1991), *The Strategy Handbook*, Oxford: Blackwell, pp. 58–60.

2. Charles Handy (1994), *The Empty Raincoat*, London: Hutchinson, pp. 49–53. See also: John R. Kimberley, Robert H. Miles and Associates (1980), *The Organisational Life Cycle: Issues in the Creation, Transformation, and Decline of Organisations*, San Francisco: Jossey-Bass Publishers.

Chapter 11

BRIEF SUMMARIES OF FIVE OTHER STUDIES

INTRODUCTION

What follows is from five very different companies, in the services sector, in retailing and in manufacturing. They had different ownership structures. That, together with the summaries below taken verbatim from their *Reports*, is as far as it is possible to go without breaking confidentiality. They are included here for two reasons. The first is lest there be any mystery about them. The second is to show that, not only is there internal consensus in the Studies, but there is consensus as between one Study and another, uninfluenced by the business they are in or by their ownership.

In all of the Studies, there was consensus that, where there was any perceived strategy, it was confined to the CEO and a few close advisers. There was a general plea for a wider, more collegial, strategic forum.

"Excitement" as a motivation for overseas diversification came up again in Study 9, as it did in Study 6.

In Study 12, the customer was seen as "the alpha and omega" of strategy, requiring a sea-change in that organisation's culture.

STUDY 8 (1989/90)

There is a strong consensus that there is no *overall Group strategy*, whatever about strategies for the individual companies. A strategic document is seen neither as a Group strategy nor as strategies for the individual companies.

Strategic decisions are perceived as being taken by the chief executive with a small group of (undefined) advisers. The decisions are perceived as mainly opportunistic.

The Group is seen as not having a *strategic capacity*, i.e., a regular pattern of work, involving the maximum appropriate number of people, against an agreed framework and goals. The reasons for this are, partly, the tight decision-making group and the fact that there is "no time" — the heads-down and get-on-with-it nature of the company.

There is no clear suggestion about how matters might be improved, except for the plea, pervasive in both *Reports*, for greater collegiality.

Thinking about *acquisitions* has been developed more than it was in the *Interim Report*. There are questions about the criteria for making acquisitions and increasing concern about the Group's capacity to manage acquisitions — management is seen as being stretched as things are.

There is a need for defined quality standards throughout the Group.

Management capability would be enhanced by some recruitment from outside. The Group should anticipate, invest and recruit ahead of need. Assessments are an effective entry point.

The chief executive said,

> "I see myself playing the role which was so aptly put by one participant, 'Admiral and not Captain'. However, I do not envisage myself as a mere figurehead who chairs meetings. I will play an arms-length executive role."

An overall view was that the Group needs to invest in its own management processes − the *how* − with the same enthusiasm as it invests in acquisitions − the *what*.

STUDY 9 (1991)

In the first interviews, there was dissatisfaction with the present strategic process: it was seen as a response to budgets or divisional procedures. It was seen as short-term, lacking perspective, focused on the present. The emphasis was on finance and marketing − little on human resources or structure. It was essentially confined to the chief executive and two advisers. It would be better formulated by a wider forum: the divisional managing directors together with the Group managers.

In the second interviews, there were some critical views on the quality of the strategy caused by a strategic process in which there was little participation.

There was a consensus that there should be a strategy committee of all those reporting to the Group CEO.

In the first interviews, the views were that the mission statement was not committed to excellence, made no mention of people and was constrained by the company's shareholders. There was a measure of support for the strategy. There was a consensus that "we should do what we know". There was a particular need for defensive or developmental action as competition increased. While there was support for the international strategy, the motivation behind it was seen as "excitement" and the constraints of the Irish market.

In the second interviews, a tendency to short-termism was noted. On overseas versus domestic expansion, the preponderant view favoured domestic. On domestic, the general view was to stick to the knitting. The strategy needed to be more sharply focused. Views on overseas acquisitions were cautious.

STUDY 10 (1993)

In the *Interim Report* there was a very strong consensus that there was no long-term plan. As the Study progressed, that view was reinforced. The simple recommendation comes from a participant:

"We need a one-year and a five-year plan."

The participant continued: that everybody agrees with, which brings us to the planning or strategic process: process precedes plans.

The views recorded in the second phase of the Study were critical of the lack of process and particularly of the various staff meetings. There was consensus that

> "we need a planning process that involves all relevant staff."

(If, at this stage of the book, the conclusion reached in Study 10 is obvious to the point of turgidity, it is well to remember that this conclusion was reached by the participants themselves, unaffected by any other Study.)

STUDY 11 (1995/96)

In this Study there were two different but equal groups of staff. First and second do not denote seniority.

There is agreement among the first group that there is no vision, strategy or direction. A plan is needed but there is uncertainty about how to do it.

There is no coherence in the views on strategic options.

Views are varied about any benchmarks against which the organisation might measure itself.

There are views from the second group on a strategic process. It must be led from the top and include beliefs, priorities, the broad picture, coherence in the top team. It will require consultation and a culture change. There will need to be a cross-cultural group (i.e. in-

cluding both groups) but there are doubts about the
other group's willingness to participate in the work.

The fact that there is at present no vision of the future, no clear (or written) strategy, is re-emphasised.
There are not explicit standards or no strategic context
in which decisions are taken.

Following this Study, a consultant on strategic process was
appointed. He was familiar with the industry. Following a
year's participative work, a strategy was agreed.

STUDY 12 (1998)

In the *Interim Report* there was consensus that there was
no strategy and that a clear strategy must come primarily from the marketplace. While there might have
been strategies at plant or divisional level, as they went
upwards they got nowhere. There was concern about
the quality of acquisitions and the subsequent investment in them. Capital expenditure decisions were
rough justice, arbitrary, unrelated to the needs of a particular plant. The company was weak at, or did not understand, marketing. There were unanswered strategic
questions.

Subsequent views reinforced the high consensus in
the *Interim Report* on the need for an overall vision and
strategic context. There were remarks that a strategy
gives freedom, is not a straitjacket. The key strategic
question was raised: *what business are we in?*

There were some strongly expressed views that the fault lay not so much in an absence of strategy as in a failure to implement strategy.

An even more pervasive issue was that strategy, the whole organisation, needed a sea-change in its culture and focus so that it was market- rather than product-driven. The customer was seen, by some, as the alpha and omega of strategy, whereas the company was seen as primarily process-orientated. Key ingredients in marketing were innovation and differentiation.

This Study led to significant changes in structure and personnel and to clarification of what constituted core and non-core businesses.

Chapter 12

CONCLUSION

*To all things there is an end
and an extremity and as soon
as they reach their culminating point,
they topple over, as they cannot
remain long in this state.*

— François Rabelais

The reasons I was asked to undertake Studies varied from CEO to CEO in the circumstances of the time. If there was a common theme it was at a general level: "I'd like you to have a look around"; or "I'd like to know what's really going on".

The Studies show how different the companies were. What is remarkable is that in all of those different organisations, the participants' most pressing issue was no shared strategic process and consequently no *shared* strategy — or even *no* strategy, at least in their eyes. My initial inclination, as I have said, was to recommend a formal process that would come up with a hard and fast plan.

Now, looking back, the Studies ended up at a somewhat different destination. Kanter wrote:

> The strategic logic guiding companies must shift
> from a producer orientation, which creates bureau-
> cracies stressing conformity and uniformity, to a
> customer orientation, which entails flexibility,
> customization and innovation.[1]

Studies did not end up with a crisp clear strategy. Perhaps there is no such thing. Studies did, however, reach
a clear identification of those issues that needed attention. Studies loosened up the organisation: things that
were once murmured as *bruit des couloirs* became common currency. And if any chief executive was in doubt
about what was going on in his organisation, at the end
of a Study he knew not only what was going on but
also what the troops thought of *him*.

Following all Studies changes were made. The most
perceptible were changes in structure and personnel.
Others were a general improvement in morale following
on greater collegiality, particularly in discussions on
strategy and direction. Collegiality, in turn, meant that
the quality and acceptance of (strategic) decisions were
improved because more brain-power was brought to
bear on those decisions and by the people who had to
carry them out.

The extent to which these good things happened de-
pended absolutely on the commitment of the chief executive. It is essential that the chief executive and the
adviser know precisely where they stand with each
other, what can be expected and what cannot be expected
from a Study. To this end, the adviser must stay closely
in touch with him (not yet her) right through a Study.

At one end of the continuum, the Studies conformed to the physician's guide: *so far as possible, do no harm.* Studies could do harm if they raised hopes that were not fulfilled. Thankfully, that never happened. At the other end, recommendations were seized with both hands by the chief executive and swiftly implemented.

A lesson I learned in the course of the Studies — and for 21 years before that in the IMI — was the futility of preaching dogma at practising managers.[2] Influences were Professor Reg Revans, the doyen, and a small number of wise men with whom I had the good fortune to work. But most of all it came from the uniquely privileged position, both in the IMI and in UCD, of having a relationship of confidentiality with many managers, mostly in Ireland, but also farther afield and in cultures as different from one another as Malaysia, Armenia and Newfoundland. I have high respect for the skill of (young) analysts, and I know the stock market does not lie — at least not in the long-term. What neither the market nor the analysts can tell is what goes on in the heads of managers faced with crisis and change, failure and success, loyalty and betrayal. And how they can be helped by a trusted outsider to see more clearly what they already know. The more you understand present reality, the more confidently you can move into the future.

Once a relationship of trust is established, there is no difficulty in telling it like it is.

My respect for the role of CEO has grown exponentially over the years. The CEO is the single person who can do the most good — and the most harm. (We did not meet in this book any CEO who did harm.) A CEO's influence is immense. The CEO may not feel that. CEOs, when they look out at the world, see so many things they can't do. Subordinates, when they look at the CEO, see real power. This is what Auden wrote about them:

> *The last word on how we may live or die*
> *Rests today with such quiet*
> *Men, working too hard in rooms that are too big*
> *Reducing to figures*
> *What is the matter, what is to be done . . .*
> *No; no one is really sorry for their*
> *Heavy gait and careworn*
> *Look, nor would they thank you if you said you were.*[3]

I am not totally objective about the chief executives in the various Studies. You cannot share their innermost thoughts with people without forming bonds of friendship. That is why, rather than sit in judgement, I gave in Chapter 3 the raw data of their subordinates' views. (I have walked away from four potential Studies either because the time was unripe or, more to the point, because I felt I would be used as the chief executive's *laidhricín* — little finger — to help him get his way. A Study's true constituency is professional managers, people who work for salaries. Where ownership of the enterprise and the role of CEO are combined in one person, there is too heady a brew for a Study to handle. I also walked away from a government department because I could not fathom what it *did*.)

There are put-downs of common sense — that it is none too common and that it does not make much sense. As was seen in the preceding pages, I have high respect for the many writers who raise our eyes above our shallow horizons. I have equally high respect for the pure stream of common sense that flows in every organisation I have worked with. Again and again managers have said to me, "It's not rocket science." Peter Drucker would agree. What Studies try to achieve is to cut through the briars and brambles so that we can see that pure stream. I am not starry-eyed. With time the briars will grow again. What we get from Studies is an *increment* of change. As I said in the *Introduction*, in established enterprises change is incremental. Bertrand de Jouvenel is more elegant:

> Only a man who has himself gone in search of truth knows how deceptive is the blaze of evidence with which a proposition may suddenly dazzle his eyes. The light soon fails, and the hunt is on again.

To coin a cliché: change is now both continuous and rapid. Studies are about helping organisations, and the individuals who constitute them, to confront that reality in a way that makes sense to *them*, thus helping *them* to change.

At the bottom of all resistance to change is a very understandable motivation: job protection.[4]

Work on the Studies has convinced me that the only enduring way to change an individual is to give him or her something different to do.

Many efforts to change an organisation fail because they miss the target.

There are three key elements in an individual's participation in an organisation: work, relationships, rewards.

Work is what an individual *does*, the way in which he or she produces outputs, reaches results. *Relationships* are with superiors, subordinates, peers; also, in a more unspecified way, with "the organisation". *Rewards* are what an individual is paid, the status accorded, the appreciation of effort, the opportunities for promotion.

The difference between work, on the one hand, and relationships and rewards, on the other, is critical. Work can give intrinsic motivation. The motivation from relationships and rewards is extrinsic. The motivation from work *can* be enduring. The motivation from relationships and rewards is episodic — "eaten bread is soon forgotten". Work *can* give *continuous* (with the emphasis on *continuous*) learning, identity, security and growth. Rewards and relationships cannot. Work can be an enduring motivator. Relationships and rewards are episodic motivators.

If people are suited to the work they do, and find it satisfying in itself, they *can* have that satisfaction ruined by an unpleasant boss, by peer jealousy, or by not being paid enough. If people are *not* suited to the work they do, and do not enjoy it for itself, the warmest personal relationships and the most generous rewards *cannot* make them enjoy it, *cannot* make them do it well, at least over any sustained period. They end up, as

Hertzberg said, being unhappy in a greater degree of comfort.[5]

An analogy may help. In playing a game, there are two objectives: enjoyment of the game itself, and winning. The game itself is what causes people to choose golf instead of sailing or soccer. It is what gives them the intrinsic satisfaction. Since games are competitive, it is also nice to win. If people lost every game they played, they would give up. On the other hand, their essential objective is not an infinite series of victories. Victories or defeats are, in fact, indicators of whether the essential objective of enjoying the game is being attained.

I have been preaching this little homily for long enough to know the danger of being misunderstood. I have heard people say, "That fellow doesn't think money is important." Contrary to popular belief, I am not so daft. Of course money is important, particularly if you don't have enough. Of course relationships are important, particularly if your boss is making life a misery.

I have had the same problem saying that the purpose of a company is not to make a profit, but to create a customer — and, *in so doing*, to make a profit so that it continues to create customers. Charles Handy puts it well:

> The principal purpose of a company is not to make a profit, full stop. It is to make a profit in order to continue to do things or make things, and to do so even better and more abundantly. To say that

profit is a means to other ends and not an end in
itself is not a semantic quibble, it is a serious moral
point. A requirement is not a purpose. In everyday
life those who make the means into ends are usually called neurotic or obsessive. We have to eat to
live, but if we live to eat we can become distorted
in more senses than one. In ethics, to mistake the
means for the ends is to be turned in on one's self,
one of the worst of sins, said St Augustine.[6]

I sat in on an interview where an unhappy employee
came to see the chief executive. He was trying to explain to his boss that he was getting no satisfaction
from his work. The boss said, "John, what on earth is
wrong with you? You're well paid. You have a job for
life. Everybody here likes you and I'd trust you with
my life. For goodness' sake, man, count your bless-
ings." The employee departed in a cloud of gloom
knowing that he had failed to communicate the heart of
the matter. When he had left, the boss threw his eyes
up to heaven and said to me, "How can you deal with
unreasonable people like that?"

The chief executive, a kindly man, was responding
as many organisations do, trying to solve problems at
the periphery rather than at the centre and, in so doing,
unconsciously encouraging conformity and dependence. People who conform are more easily managed —
at least in the short run.

You won't get change simply by being nice to people
or paying them more. The heart of the matter is what
they do. Change that and you change the people: their
purpose, their skills, their attitudes. Change the people

and you change the organisation. *Then* the rewards follow.

Of course, it's not that simple. You can't make every job in an organisation fit the aspirations of every individual even in the best of times. Following a fundamental change, there will always be people who either can't or won't adapt — and with whom the organisation may have to part company. It would be misplaced *comhthrom Féinne* to keep them on. It is better to replace them lest their misery becomes infectious.

However, it behoves us to look at how these people got there in the first place. Blaming *them* for being there is as useful as a slammed door in a domestic argument. It gives momentary satisfaction. It solves nothing. If we are to avoid facing exactly the same problems next time round, we have to look a little deeper.

I have heard the joke that there are two kinds of people: those who think there are two kinds of people and those who don't. But see if what follows finds an echo in your experience.

Pirates live their lives in single dimensions with work divorced from personal values, from family, from leisure, from social obligations. Their work is often at odds with what they personally need. This splitting of their job from all other aspects of their lives will manifest itself in rigidity, selfishness and hostility. The hostility is unconscious and usually well disguised.

Builders see their work as giving purpose and significance to their whole lives. Their work is congruent with their personal needs. They do not make worse the historic conflict between personal and organisation needs and do not exploit the organisation for short-term benefits to the organisation's long-term damage. Why? Because they do not have the hostility that comes from the sycophantic way the pirate operates.

Sycophants feel they must agree with their boss to get ahead and, in hiding their true feelings, build up hostility against both the boss and the company. The organisation, in turn, invites subservience.

Pirates evaluate themselves quantitatively: their salary bracket; how much power they have; what car they drive; what kind of house they live in; even, eventually, what kind of friends they have. Since they live their whole lives quantitatively, their effects on the organisation are a lack of spontaneity and creativity, leading to rigidity and bureaucracy, to seeing the organisation as an index game. Measurement becomes divorced from objectives and objectives are lost in a maze of irrelevant measurement.

Builders, on the other hand, evaluate their work qualitatively. They think of personal growth rather than hierarchical status. They see social responsibility not as part of a job description but as part of their humanity. Because the measures are more qualitative, builders understand more than pirates do. They may be less effective, perhaps, in terms of the organisation's short-term goals — because of lack of concern for immediate results — but they are more valuable to the organisation's long-term flexibility and, therefore, survival.

Success for pirates is always empty. They reach the top of the ladder and they can only go down. Since they have been one-dimensional, all aspects of their lives decline. Fame lacks intimacy — hence the loneliness. The organisation is then stuck with an obsolete person rather than merely an obsolete talent. Obsolete people have nothing to fall back on. They defend their obsolescence with slogans.

For the builders, success is continually experienced. Their fate is not decline — it is unfinished experience. The core dimension of their lives remains. They are constantly useful. They do not become embittered or sycophantic. They remain a healthy asset.

The relationships pirates have with other people are antiseptic. Conflict is suppressed until it breaks out in trauma. This trauma is then coldly analysed, polarised by intellectual arguments and finally degenerates into win-lose situations. The consequent cover-up is more human relations technology: not conversation but "communicating", not honesty but "levelling" with one another. The result is to reinforce conflict and a win-lose system.

Builders have natural, human relationships and take conflicts in their stride, not analysing but experiencing, adding to their personal growth, reaching out in conflict for further personal enrichment.

The argument is that there *are* two discernible kinds of people: pirates and builders, and one of them can be disastrous when change is necessary. No better people than pirates to protect their jobs.

However, when it comes to our taking decisions about whom to select, the problem lies less in our recognition of these psychological types than in our distorted view of what is good for the organisation facing change. We sometimes select people we can't stand (as people) because of a misguided belief that a certain kind of driven madness will impel the organisation in a sensible direction. We home in on the impulsion and neglect the direction, like the Ferrari owner with a faulty map who gets more quickly to the wrong place.

―――――――

A conference of the International Academy of Management in Barcelona was described as "a crashing of shibboleths as dogma gave way to pragmatism".[7]

In the *Introduction* I said that there was a movement in management literature from a directive, this-is-how-you-do-it approach to a humbler, more holistic one. It is brick on brick. Everything that has gone before is not a shibboleth and pragmatism does not now reign supreme. Contrary to Henry Ford's view, history is not more or less bunk. To believe that would be a true dumbing-down. In Barcelona, my distinguished colleagues were falling into the trap of false dichotomies.

Just as we need openness to new knowledge, so do we need to remember the lessons of the past. Put the other way around: effective strategies need not squander out heritage, but they have to be unchained from those traditions, values and behaviour whose usefulness has disappeared. Talleyrand said: "In all one's actions one must have in mind the future and the past."

We need both freedom and order. Without freedom you get recidivist organisations. Without order you get anarchy.

In our market or mixed economy, people are free to make their own decisions within a known framework established by law. This framework is based on the conviction that there is an inherent benefit to the individuals in our society in favouring the free as against the authoritarian way of doing things. This is a form deeply rooted in the worth of the individual. To us, the individual — not a class or a state or an organisation — is the central element. The individual's consent is the essence of our political life. The individual's happiness is the essence of our economic philosophy. The individual's salvation is the essence of our spiritual order. The individual's freedom is the ultimate test of all we value.

Freedom is not licence; nor is it libertarianism; nor, worse, a modish Dublin 4 liberalism. It was not even as an element in the happiness of the individual that, throughout history, lofty spirits vaunted it. It was, rather, because freedom consecrated the dignity of the human personality. It saved the individual from playing the merely instrumental role to which authority tends ever to reduce people.

Those laws are best that require least reinforcement: laws that are rooted in the moral habits of the citizens and enjoy their respect. We need to distinguish between laws and commands. Laws are impersonal rules, general, disinterested, usually negative in form: "Thou shalt not kill." Laws are observed. Commands are obeyed. To live under the rule of law is to be a citizen. To live under commandment is to be a subject.

If freedom is so fundamental to us, is it not reasonable to suggest that the organisations that maximise individual freedom will be the effective ones, flexible, responsive at a time of change?

And is it not equally reasonable to suggest that organisations that encourage conformity and dependence will be dull and unresponsive to change?

This is where order comes in. With order goes personal responsibility. Order is about knowing where you stand, what is expected of you, where your organisation is going. It is about having a continuous flow of *information* — knowledge — so that you can take your own decisions within accepted limits. Order is about clarity. The opposite of clarity is ignorance, uncertainty and lack of confidence, leading to stasis.

My favourite Thurber cartoon is an eager swain saying to the object of his ardour, "What do you want to be inscrutable *for*, Marcia?"

I have never worked in an organisation that did not have communication problems and that includes the organisations in this book. It was not so much a desire for inscrutability (though I have seen the most banal memos headed "eyes only"), rather it was the aloofness we discussed earlier, the reluctance of some CEOs to get out and mix it with the troops, to listen and argue, even to change their minds occasionally, genuinely to share with their colleagues their vision of the future, the actions necessary to attain it — and the actions or behaviour that could inhibit or damage the organisation and that could not be tolerated.

We are living through an information revolution. It is dissonant to have expectations in our civil life greatly at variance with what we can expect in our organisational life. A rule I've had in the Studies is never to underestimate people's intelligence and never to overestimate their information. The chief executive in Study 6 (p. 204) said, "When I read the *Reports* I was shocked sometimes at how much ignorance there was." Well, if the pupil has not learned, the teacher has not taught.

A recent Conference Board report said that knowledge *management* was being hailed as "the next strategic imperative after total quality management (TQM) and business process reengineering (BPR)":

> Some organisations see it as little more than information management while others see it as something far more complex, involving management of knowledge in all its forms. Proponents of knowledge management . . . believe that it is a source of sustainable competitive advantage . . . Knowledge management has many different definitions but is generally taken to be the distribution, creation, sharing and application of knowledge.[8]

I walked into the splendid office of the chief executive of a very large company. He was so engrossed in the report he was reading that he did not look up. I was left standing. Then he threw down the report and said with some feeling, "That bloody analyst knows more about my company than I do."

In my erstwhile youth, when I had the temerity to "teach" management, I used to talk about the *Law of Requisite Variety*. It rolled off the tongue and gave me an ephemeral authority. But it made sense: a complex organism cannot survive in a simple environment and a simple organism cannot survive in a complex environment.

There can hardly be an organisation now that does not subsist in a complex environment — global, inter-related, discontinuous — an environment that is not amenable to simple solutions. Mature managers know that. Perhaps one-minute-managers still search for slogans.

I have heard managers in moments of weariness hanker after the good old days, when life seemed more predictable, when people did what they were told and minded their own business.

It was the late Marshall McLuhan, author of *The Medium is the Massage*, who said, "You can't go home any more." It was a graffito in the toilet of New York's Grand Central Station that reminded us: "Nostalgia kills."

Whose heart does not beat a little faster at the words of the chairman of the board in the *New Yorker* cartoon:

> And though last year, as in previous years, your
> company had to deal with spiralling labour costs,
> exorbitant interest rates, and unconscionable gov-
> ernment interference, management was able once

more, through a combination of deceptive marketing practices, false advertising, and price fixing, to show a profit which, in all modesty, can only be called excessive.

Those days are gone. Anyone who relies on the past as a guide to the future might well heed the admonition in the Preface to the Book of Common Prayer: "There was never any thing by the wit of man so well devised, or so sure established, which in continuance of time hath not been corrupted." Karl Marx, who probably put little store in the Book of Common Prayer, though it has lasted rather longer than *Das Kapital*, said: "The tradition of all the dead generations weighs like a nightmare on the brain of the living."

It may be hard to slough off the dead though still protective skin of old attitudes and beliefs. Like the King, we may announce that we can repair Humpty Dumpty, but we need more horses and more men. We may try to solve problems with our existing tools in their old context.

The future cannot be met only with systems and techniques. While we need continually to push the frontiers of knowledge, much of management is art. Effective management is a combination of knowledge and intuition, of position and personality, of environmental constraints and human will, of time and chance.

It is a high form of leadership, for it seeks to combine the act — the getting something done — with the meaning behind the act.

Effective managers have to synthesise, to integrate different and conflicting theories and themes. They have to engage issues on the level of fact and feeling, to address questions that lie in the overlap between science and philosophy — between the tangible and the intangible. And they must overcome a lack of adequate theory to assist them in integrating talent, task, values and technology. Finally, having broken free from the womb of either/or thinking, they must work in the knowledge that they are beset not by stark choices, but by continual paradoxes. And, as was said in Study 4, there is no end to the day. Since we can seldom *find* it, what is needed is a constant *search* for truth, constant questioning, constant experimentation, a determination to keep asking why. Robert Louis Stevenson told us there was no El Dorado, that to *travel hopefully is better than to arrive, and the true success is to labour.* The reward may be to get it right more often than we get it wrong. That is enough and that is what managers know.

Notes

1.   Rosabeth Moss Kanter (1997), *Frontiers of Management*, Boston: Harvard Business School Press, p. 27.

2.   "The enterprise where we work is far and away the most significant business school that managers ever attend." Gordon Wills (1993), *Your Enterprise School of Management*, Bradford: MCB University Press, p. 9.

3. W.H. Auden, "The Managers", from Ralph Windle (1994), *The Poetry of Business Life*, San Francisco: Berrett-Koehler Publishers, Inc., pp. 64 and 66.

4. Within the limits of this book, we cannot discuss the trade unions whose sole purpose is job protection (and enhancement). Their agenda is essentially a political one. In Ireland, they face deep change in the private sector and while, at the top of the trade union movement, liberal and enlightened statements are made, there is a worrying gap with the workers on the shop floor and their immediate champions, the shop stewards. Faced with the inexorable onslaught of competition in the private sector, trade unions have retreated to the high ground of the State sector: monopoly public utilities and health or education. There they strike, not against the employers, but against the public — patients, parents, householders, travellers — in the certain knowledge that no Irish government will take on a trade union — at least not for long. But change they will have to, just as enterprise has to change. The change will be turbulent and no one can be sure of its destination. Their power base is shrinking and that is not a cause for sweetness and light. John Monks, leader of Britain's Trade Union Congress, said, "Trade unions are like gorillas in the forest, suffering from a shrinking habitat." See also Ivor Kenny (1984), *Government and Enterprise in Ireland*, Dublin: Gill and Macmillan, pp. 61–70.

5. Frederick Hertzberg (1975), "One More Time: How Do You Motivate Employees?", *Harvard Business Review — On Management*, London: Heineman, pp. 361–76.

6. Charles Handy (1994), *The Empty Raincoat*, London: Hutchinson, p. 136.

7. International Academy of Management (1987), Barcelona Conference, *Proceedings* (private circulation).

8. The Conference Board Europe (1998), *Knowledge Management: Creating Organisational Value*, report on a conference in Brussels, 15–16 September. See also: David J. Skyrme (1998), "Fact or Fad? Ten Shifts in Knowledge Management", *Knowledge Management Review*, Vol. 3, pp. 6–7.

SELECT BIBLIOGRAPHY

The bibliography is called select because it lists only books on my shelves, books I have actually read. It has no pretension to comprehensiveness. However, if you were to compare the bibliographies in books by authorities, what is surprising is the number of other books not listed. (You would also get an insight into what they think of one another. For instance in Michael Porter's 1980 book, *Competitive Strategy*, Mintzberg is not mentioned once in the bibliography.) In the early 1950s I was finishing a master's thesis in the Reading Room of the British Museum. With its marvellous resources I felt I had read everything there was to read. Late in the day I came across a footnote which referred to Luigi Sturzo's "definitive" book on my subject. I had never heard of Mr Sturzo.

Research has confirmed what we know instinctively: that managers buy books but rarely read them to the end.

> Management Theory, more than any other branch of academia, is propelled by two primal human instincts: fear and greed. It is usually one of these two emotions that persuades a middle manager at

Heathrow Airport to pick up yet another book on
leadership . . . (Micklethwait and Wooldridge, *The
Witch Doctors*, p. 9.)

One can hardly blame managers for not struggling on
to the last page. Books on strategy, in particular, can be
facile or turgid. The antithesis of the theoreticians
would be Peter V. Simpson et al. (1996), *Business Planning Success*, Bishop's Stortford: Dynamic Pathways
(UK) Ltd. The cover, which features a handsome tie-
less gentleman, says, capitals and all, "In One Day,
Build a Strategic Plan that Secures Capital". On the
other hand, the first sentence in Ray Wild's book (see
below) reads, "This may be one of the most authorita-
tive books on management ever published . . ."

I have marked with an asterisk those books or arti-
cles I found particularly relevant.

Ackoff, Russell L. (1981), *Creating the Corporate Future*, London: Wiley.

Adams, John D. and Sabina A. Spencer (1986), *Transforming
Leadership*, Virginia: Miles River Press.

Alkhafaji, Abbass, F. (1993), "Privatisation: an Overview",
Journal of Organisational Change Management, Vol. 6, No. 3.

*Ansoff, Igor (1984), *Implementing Strategic Management*,
Englewood Cliffs, NJ: Prentice Hall.

Argenti, John (1980), *Practical Corporate Planning*, London:
Allen & Unwin.

*Argyris, C. (1985), *Strategy, Change and Defensive Routines*, London: Pitman.

Barnard, C. (1948), *Organisation and Management*, Cambridge, MA: Harvard University Press.

Barr, Nicholas (1987), *The Economics of the Welfare State*, London: Weidenfeld and Nicolson.

*Barron, Frank and Dermot Egan (n.d.), *Leaders and Innovators in Irish Management*, Dublin: The Human Sciences Committee of the Irish National Productivity Committee.

Barsoux, Jean-Louis (1989), "Management Work — Telling It Like It Is", *European Management Journal*, Vol. 7, No. 2.

Bartlett, Christopher A. and Sumantra Ghoshal (1994), "Beyond Strategy to Purpose", *Harvard Business Review*, November–December.

Bass, G.M. (1981), *Stogdills Handbook of Leadership*, New York: Free Press.

Bates, D.L. and John E. Dillard, Junior (1993), "Generating Strategic Thinking Through Multi-Level Teams", *Long Range Planning*, Vol. 26, No. 5.

Beatty, Jack (1998), *The World According to Drucker: the Life and Work of the World's Greatest Management Thinker*, London: Orion Business Books.

Beer, Michael, Russell A. Eisenstat and Bert Spector (1990), "Why Change Programmes Don't Produce Change", *Harvard Business Review*, November–December.

Bell, Daniel (1965), *The End of Ideology: on the Exhaustion of Political Ideas in the 50s*, New York: The Free Press.

*Bennis, Warren and Bert Nanus (1985), *Leaders*, New York: Harper & Row.

Bennis, Warren (1989), *On Becoming a Leader*, London: Business Books.

Bennis, Warren (1990), *Why Leaders Can't Lead*, Oxford: Jossey-Bass Publishers.

Bennis, Warren and Joan Goldsmith (1997), *Learning to Lead*, London: Nicholas Brealey Publishing.

*Berlew, David E. and Douglas T. Hall (1966), "The Sociali-sation of Managers: Effects of Expectations on Performance", *Administrative Science Quarterly*, Vol. 11, No. 2.

Bonner, Kevin, Secretary, Department of Enterprise and Em-ployment (1995), "Government and Business — Antagonists or Partners?", Address to Irish Management Institute Con-ference, 31 March.

Bosanquet, Nick (1983), *After the New Right*, London: Heine-mann.

Brittan, Samuel (1995), *Capitalism with a Human Face*, Alder-shot: Edward Elgar Publishing Limited.

Campbell, Colin and George J. Szablowski (1979), *The Super-Bureaucrats: Structure and Behaviour in Central Agencies*, To-ronto: Macmillan of Canada.

Carland, J.W., F. Hoy, W.R. Boulton and J.A.C. Carland (1984), "Differentiating Entrepreneurs from Small Business Owners: a Conceptualisation", *Academy of Management Re-view*, Vol. 9, No. 2.

Carlson, Sune (1951), *Executive Behaviour: A Study of the Workload and Working Methods of Managing Directors*, Stock-holm: Strömberg.

Carsrud, A.L., K.W. Olm and G.G. Eddy (1986), "Entrepre-neurship: Research in Quest of a Paradigm", in D.L. Sexton and R.W. Smilor (eds.), *The Art and Science of Entrepreneur-ship*, Cambridge, MA: Ballinger.

Casson, Mark (1982), *The Entrepreneur: an Economic Theory*, Oxford: Martin Robertson.

Chandler, A.D. (1962), *Strategy and Structure*, Massachusetts: MIT Press.

Chapman, Lesley (1978), *Your Disobedient Servant*, London: Chatto and Windus.

Chell, E. (1988), "The Entrepreneurial Personality: a Review and Some Theoretical Developments" in Elizabeth J. Chell and Jean M. Haworth, *Explorations of the Entrepreneurial Personality*, Paper presented to the Second Workshop on Recent Research on Entrepreneurship, European Institute for Advanced Studies in Management, Vienna, 5–6 December.

Clavell, James, (ed.) (1983), *The Art of War, Sun Tsu*, New York: Doubleday Dell.

Clifford, Donald K., Jr. and Richard E. Cavanagh (1985), *The Winning Performance: How America's High-Growth Midsize Companies Succeed*, Toronto: Bantam Books.

*Collins, James C. and Jerry I. Porras (1994), *Built to Last, Successful Habits of Visionary Companies*, London: Random House.

Conference Board Europe (1998), *Knowledge Management: Creating Organisational Value*, report on a conference in Brussels, 15–16 September.

Convery, Frank and Moore McDowell (eds.) (1990), *Privatisation: Issues of Principle and Implementation in Ireland*, Dublin: Gill and Macmillan.

Covey, Stephen R. (1992), *The Seven Habits of Highly Effective People: Powerful Lessons in Personal Change*, London: Simon & Schuster.

Crainer, Stuart (1996), *Leaders on Leadership*, Corby: The Institute of Management.

Crozier, Michel, avec Bruno Tilliette (1995), *La Crise de l'Intelligence, Essai sur l'Impuissance des Élites à se Réformer*, Paris: InterEditions.

Curran, J. et al. (eds.) (1986), *The Survival of the Small Firm, Volume 1: The Economics of Survival and Entrepreneurship*, Aldershot: Gower.

Dalton, Melvin (1959), *Men Who Manage*, New York: Wiley.

*Dauphinais, William and Colin Price (eds.) (1998), *Straight from the CEO: The World's Top Business Leaders Reveal Ideas that Every Manager Can Use*, London: Nicholas Brealey Publishing.

Davies, Adrian (1991), *Strategic Leadership: Making Corporate Plans Work*, London: Woodhead-Faulkner.

Davis, Stanley M. (1983), "Management Models for the Future", *New Management*, Vol. 1, Spring.

de Closets, François (1982), *Toujours Plus!*, Paris: Bernard Grasset.

Dillon-Malone, Patrick (1970), *An Analysis of Marketing*, Dublin: Irish Management Institute.

Dixon, Norman F. (1983), *On the Psychology of Military Incompetence*, London: Futura.

Donaldson, Gordon and Jay W. Lorsch (1983), *Decision-Making at the Top: the Shaping of Strategic Direction*, New York: Basic Books, Inc.

Drucker, Peter F. (1968), *The Effective Executive*, London: Heinemann.

Drucker, Peter F. (1969), *The Age of Discontinuity: Guidelines to Our Changing Society*, London: Heinemann.

Drucker, Peter F. (1989), *The New Realities*, Oxford: Heinemann Professional Publishing.

Drucker, Peter F. (1992), *Managing for the Future*, Oxford: Butterworth-Heinemann Limited.

Dunlop, John T. (ed.) (1980), *Business and Public Policy*, Cambridge, MA: Harvard University Press.

Eccles, Tony (1994), *Succeeding with Change: Implementing Action-Driven Strategies*, London: McGraw-Hill Book Company.

*European Institute for Advanced Studies in Management, European Foundation for Management Development (1981), *Facing Realities, The Report of the European Societal Strategy Project*, Brussels.

Evans, P. and Y. Doz (1989), "The Dualist Organization", *Human Resource Management in International Firms: Change, Globalization, Innovation*, London: Macmillan.

Fanning, Ronan (1978), *The Irish Department of Finance, 1922–58*, Dublin: Institute of Public Administration.

Fayol, Henri (1925 Reprint), "Administration industrielle et générale — prévoyance, organisation, coordination, contrôle", *Bulletin de la Societé de l'Industrie Minérale*. Republished in book form, Paris: Dunod.

Fenn, Dan H., Jr., Donald Grunewald and Robert N. Katz (1966), *Business Decision-Making and Government Policy: Cases in Business and Government*, Englewood Cliffs, NJ: Prentice Hall, Inc.

Figgis, J.N. and R.V. Laurence (eds.) (1907), *Lord John Acton: The History of Freedom and Other Essays*, London: Macmillan.

Finlay, Fergus (1998), *Snakes & Ladders*, Dublin: New Island Books.

Fogarty, M.P. (1973), *Irish Entrepreneurs Speak for Themselves*, Dublin: ESRI Broadsheet No. 8, December.

Foster, Richard (1986), *Innovation: the Attacker's Advantage*, London: Macmillan.

Friedman, Milton and Rose Friedman (1980), *Free to Choose*, London: Secker and Warburg.

Fry, Joseph N. and J. Peter Killing (1986), *Strategic Analysis and Action*, Scarborough, Ontario: Prentice-Hall Canada Inc.

Gardner, Howard (1995), *Leading Minds: an Anatomy of Leadership*, London: HarperCollins.

Garelli, Stéphane (ed.) (1998), *The World Competitiveness Yearbook 1998*, Lausanne: IMD, May.

Gilmour, Ian (1969), *The Body Politic*, London: Hutchinson.

*Goldsmith, Walter and David Clutterbuck (1984), *The Winning Streak: Britain's Top Companies Reveal Their Formulas for Success*, London: Weidenfeld and Nicolson.

*Gorman, Liam (1989), "Corporate Culture", *Management Decision*, Vol. 27, No. 1.

Gorman, Liam, Ruth Handy, Tony Moynihan and Roderick Murphy (1974), *Managers in Ireland*, Dublin: Irish Management Institute.

Government of Ireland (1993), *Employment Through Enterprise: The Response of the Government to the Moriarty Task Force on the Implementation of the Culliton Report*, Dublin: The Stationery Office.

Gray, John (1993), *Beyond the New Right: Markets, Government and the Common Environment*, London: Routledge.

Grieve Smith, John (1985), *Business Strategy*, Oxford: Basil Blackwell.

*Hamel, Gary (1998), "Strategy Innovation and the Question for Value", *Sloan Management Review*, Winter.

*Hamel, Gary and C.K. Prahalad (1994), *Competing for the Future*, Massachusetts: Harvard Business School Press.

*Handy, Charles (1976), *Understanding Organisations*, Harmondsworth: Penguin Books Limited.

*Handy, Charles (1978), *Gods of Management: Who They Are, How They Work, and Why They Will Fail*, London: Pan Books.

Handy, Charles (1990), *Inside Organisations*, London: BBC Books.

*Handy, Charles (1994), *The Empty Raincoat: Making Sense of the Future*, London: Hutchinson.

Handy, Charles (1997), *The Hungry Spirit: Beyond Capitalism, a Quest for Purpose in the Modern World*, London: Hutchinson.

Harrison, Roger (1983), "Strategies for a New Age", *Human Resource Management*, Fall.

Harvard Business Review (1975), *On Management*, London: Heinemann.

Harvey, Brian, Stephen Smith and Barry Wilkinson (1984), *Managers and Corporate Social Policy: Private Solutions to Public Problems?*, London: The Macmillan Press Limited.

Harvey, Gerry B. (1988), *The Abilene Paradox and Other Meditations on Management*, Toronto: Lexington Books.

*Hay, Michael and Peter Williamson (1991), *The Strategy Handbook*, Oxford: Blackwell.

Hayek, F.A. (1979), *The Road to Serfdom*, London: Routledge and Keegan Paul.

Heald, David (1983), *Public Expenditure*, Oxford: Martin Robertson.

*Heclo, Hugh and Aaron Wildavsky (1981), *The Private Government of Public Money*, London, Macmillan.

Heilbroner, Robert L. (1972), *The Economic Problem*, Englewood Cliffs, NJ: Prentice Hall.

*Herzberg, Frederick (1966), *Work and the Nature of Man*, Cleveland: The World Publishing Company.

Herzberg, F. (1976), *Managerial Choice: To Be Efficient and To Be Human*, Irwin: Dow Jones.

*Hesselbein, Frances (1996), Marshall Goldsmith and Richard Beckhard (eds.), *The Leader of the Future*, San Francisco: Jossey-Bass Publishers.

Horton, Thomas R. (1986), *What Works for Me*, New York: Random House.

Hutton, Will (1996), *The State We're In*, London: Vintage.

International Academy of Management (1987), Barcelona Conference, *Proceedings*, September (private circulation).

*Jaques, Elliott (1956), *The Measurement of Responsibility*, London: Tavistock.

*Jaques, Elliott (1990), "In Praise of Hierarchy", *Harvard Business Review*, January–February.

Johnson, Gerry and Kevan Scholes (1984), *Exploring Corporate Strategy*, London: Prentice Hall International.

Joyce, Brian (1998), "Public Transport — Facing Reality", address to the Chartered Institute of Transport, Dublin, 17 November.

Judson, Arnold S. (1990), *Making Strategy Happen: Transforming Plans Into Reality*, Oxford: Basil Blackwell.

Kane, Aidan (1998), "Privatisation: The Right Policy, the Wrong Reasons", *The Sunday Business Post*, 9 August.

*Kanter, Rosabeth Moss (1989), *When Giants Learn to Dance: Mastering the Challenges of Strategy, Management and Careers in the 1990s*, London: Simon & Schuster.

Kanter, Rosabeth Moss (1997), *Frontiers of Management*, Boston: Harvard Business School Press.

Kenny, Ivor (1954), *Church and State in Western Europe*, M.A. Dissertation.

Kenny, Ivor (Chairman) (1983), *Lifelong Learning: Report of the Commission on Adult Education*, Dublin: The Stationery Office.

Kenny, Ivor (1984), "Business, Politics and Society", *The Future of Management Education*, Aldershot: Gower.

Kenny, Ivor (1984), *Government and Enterprise in Ireland*, Dublin: Gill and Macmillan.

Kenny, Ivor (1986), "Consultancy Revisited", *Irish Marketing Review*, Vol. 1, Spring.

Kenny, Ivor (1987), *In Good Company*, Dublin: Gill and Macmillan.

Kenny, Ivor (1988), "Management and Mythology", Centenary Address to the Institute of Chartered Accountants, April.

Kenny, Ivor (1991), *Out on Their Own*, Dublin: Gill and Macmillan.

Kenny, Ivor (1994), *Boardroom Practice* (Second Edition), Dublin: UCD.

Kenny, Ivor (1994), "The Truth, the Whole Truth and Nothing but the Truth?", Talk to Literati Club, London: 22 November.

Keuning, Doede and Wilfred Opheij (1994), *Delayering Organisations: How to Beat Bureaucracy and Create a Flexible and Responsive Organisation*, London: Financial Times Pitman Publishing.

Kilby, P.M. (1971), *Entrepreneurship and Economic Development*, New York: The Force Press.

Kimberly, John R., Robert H. Miles and Associates (1980), *The Organisation Life Cycle: Issues in the Creation, Transformation and Decline of Organisations*, San Francisco: Jossey-Bass Publishers.

Koontz, Harold (1980), "The Management Theory Jungle Revisited", *Academy of Management Review*.

Kotter, John P. (1985), *Power and Influence: Beyond Formal Authority*, New York: The Free Press.

*Kotter, John P. (1986), *The General Managers*, New York: The Free Press.

Kotter, John P. (1988), *The Leadership Factor*, New York: The Free Press.

Kotter, John P. (1990), "What Leaders Really Do", *Harvard Business Review*, May–June.

Kristol, Irving (1978), *Two Cheers for Capitalism*, New York: Basic Books.

Lane, Robert (1991), *The Market Experience*, Cambridge University Press.

Leonard-Barton, Dorothy (1995), *Wellsprings of Knowledge: Building and Sustaining the Sources of Innovation*, Boston: Harvard Business School Press.

Levitt, Theodore (1976), "Marketing Myopia", *Harvard Business Review: On Management*, London: Heinemann.

*Leys, Simon (1997), *The Analects of Confucius*, New York: W.W. Norton.

Lieberman, Ira W. (1993), "Privatisation: an Overview", *The Columbia Journal of World Business*, Spring.

Lindblom, Charles E. (1977), *Politics and Markets: the World's Political-Economic Systems*, New York: Basic Books, Inc.

Linowes, David F. (1973), *Strategies for Survival: Using Business Know-How to Make Our Social System Work*, New York: AMACOM.

Lundberg, Craig C. (1990), "Surfacing Organisational Culture", *Journal of Management Psychology*, Vol. 5, No. 4.

*McGregor, Douglas (1960), *The Human Side of Enterprise*, New York: McGraw Hill.

McGregor, Douglas (1967), *The Professional Manager*, New York: McGraw Hill.

Maljers, F.A. (1990), "Strategic Planning and Intuition in Unilever", *Long-Range Planning*, Vol. 23, No. 2.

*Margerison, Charles (1988), *Managerial Consulting Skills: A Practical Guide*, Aldershot: Gower.

*Maslow, Abraham H. (1968), *Towards a Psychology of Being*, New York: D. van Nostrand Company Incorporated.

Maslow, Abraham, H. (1970), *Motivation and Personality*, New York: Harper and Row.

Meenan, James (1970), *The Irish Economy Since 1922*, Liverpool University Press.

Meredith, G.G., R.E. Nelson and P.A. Neck (1982), *The Practice of Entrepreneurship*, Geneva: International Labour Office.

Metzger, Robert O. (1990), "With So Many Consultants, Why Aren't We Better?", *Journal of Management Consulting*, July.

*Micklethwait, J. and A. Wooldridge (1996), *The Witch Doctors*, London: Heinemann.

Minogue, Kenneth (1985), *Alien Powers, The Pure Theory of Ideology*, New York: St. Martin's Press.

Mintzberg, Henry (1973), *The Nature of Managerial Work*, New York: Harper and Row.

Mintzberg, Henry (1987), "The Strategy Concept 1: Five Ps for Strategy", *California Review*, Autumn.

Mintzberg, Henry (1987), "Crafting Strategy", *Harvard Business Review*, July/August.

Mintzberg, Henry (1990), "The Manager's Job: Folklore and Fact", *Harvard Business Review*, March-April.

*Mintzberg, Henry (1994), *The Rise and Fall of Strategic Planning*, London: Prentice Hall.

Morello, Gabriele (ed.) (1994), "Time Perception in Marketing and Social Research", *Proceedings* of the ISIDA Seminar, 18–20 May, Palermo: ISIDA.

Morgan, Gareth (1987), *Riding the Cutting-Edge of Change*, York University: Faculty of Administrative Studies.

Murray, John A. (1981), "In Search of Entrepreneurship", *Journal of Irish Business and Administrative Research*, Vol. 3.

Nadler, David A. and Michael L. Tushman (1990), "Beyond the Charismatic Leader: Leadership and Organisational Change", *California Management Review*, Winter.

Newman, Jeremiah (1987), *Puppets of Utopia: Can Irish Democracy be Taken for Granted?*, Dublin: Four Courts Press.

Novak, Michael (1984), *Freedom with Justice*, San Francisco: Harper & Row.

O'Connor, Joyce and Mary Lyons (1983), *Enterprise – The Irish Approach*, Dublin: The Industrial Development Authority, Publication Series Paper 7.

O'Farrell, Patrick (1986), *Entrepreneurs and Industrial Change: the Process of Change in Irish Manufacturing*, Dublin: Irish Management Institute.

*Ohmae, Kenichi (1990), *The Borderless World: Power and Strategy in the Interlinked Economy*, London: Collins.

Parker, David and Steve Martin (1993), "Testing Time for Privatisation", *Management Today*, August.

*Pascale, Richard (1991), *Managing on the Edge: How Successful Companies Use Conflict to Stay Ahead*, London: Penguin Books.

Perry, Chad (1990), "After Further Sightings of the Heffalump", *Journal of Managerial Psychology*, Vol. 5, No. 2.

Peters, Tom and Robert H. Waterman, Jr. (1982), *In Search of Excellence*, New York: Harper & Row.

Peters, Tom and Nancy Austin (1985), *A Passion for Excellence: the Leadership Difference*, New York: Random House.

Peters, Tom (1987), *Thriving on Chaos*, New York: Alfred A. Knopf.

Peters, J.T., K.R. Hammond and D.A. Summers (1974), "A Note on Intuitive versus Analytic Thinking", *Organisational Behaviour and Human Performance*, Vol. 12.

Pirsig, Robert M. (1983), *Zen and the Art of Motor Cycle Maintenance*, Corgi Books.

Pocock, C.C., (chairman) (1977), *Report of the Committee on Educational and Training Needs of European Managers*, Brussels: European Foundation for Management Development.

Porter, Michael E. (1980), *Competitive Strategy: Techniques for Analysing Industries and Competitors*, New York: The Free Press.

Poulsen, P. Thygesen (1993), *The Paradox of Success*, LEGO — en virksomhed og dens sjael, Copenhagen: Schultz.

Redwood, John (1980), *Public Enterprise in Crisis: the Future for the Nationalised Industries*, Oxford: Basil Blackwell.

*Revans, Reginald W. (1982), *The Origins and Growth of Action Learning*, Bromley: Chartwell-Bratt.

Rhenman, Eric (1973), *Organisation Theory for Long-Range Planning*, New York: Wiley.

Ricards, Tudor (1985), *Stimulating Innovation: a Systems Approach*, London: Frances Pinter.

Ritchie, Berry and Walter Goldsmith (1988), *The New Elite*, London: Penguin Books.

Roberts, Wess (1989), *The Leadership Secrets of Atilla the Hun*, New York: Warner Books.

Ryan, Louden (1982), "Prospects for the 80s", *The Economic and Social State of the Nation*, Dublin: Economic and Social Research Institute.

Sathe, Vijay (1983), "Implications of Corporate Culture: a Manager's Guide to Action", *Organisational Dynamics*, Autumn.

Schein, Edgar H. (1985), *Organisational Culture and Leadership*, San Francisco: Jossey-Bass.

Schein, Edgar H. (1993), "How Can Organisations Learn Faster? The Challenge of Entering the Green Room", *Sloane Management Review*, Winter.

Schön, Donald A. (1987), *Educating the Reflective Practitioner*, San Francisco: Jossey-Bass Publishers.

Schumacher, E.F. (1973), *Small is Beautiful*, London: Blonde & Briggs.

Schwartz, Peter (1991), *The Art of the Long View*, London: Century Business.

*Senge, Peter M. (1990), *The Fifth Discipline*, New York: Doubleday Currency.

Shapiro, Eileen C., Robert G. Eccles and Trina L. Soske (1993), "Consulting: Has the Solution Become Part of the Problem?", *Sloan Management Review*, Summer.

Shonfield, Andrew (1982), *The Use of Public Power*, Oxford University Press.

Simon, H.A. (1987), "Making Management Decisions: The Role of Intuition and Emotion", *Academy of Management Executive*, Vol. 1, February.

Simon, William E. (1978), *A Time for Truth*, New York: McGraw-Hill Book Company.

Sims, David (1993), "Coping with Misinformation", *Management Decision*, Vol. 31, No. 5.

Skinner, B.F. (1972), *Beyond Freedom and Dignity*, London: Jonathan Cape.

Skyrme, David J. (1998), "Fact or Fad? Ten Shifts in Knowledge Management", *Knowledge Management Review*, Vol. 3, pp. 6–7.

Smurfit, Michael (n.d.), *The International Growth of an Irish Enterprise*, The Dillon-Malone Lecture, Dublin: Jefferson Smurfit Group PLC.

Steiner, George A. (1983), *The New CEO*, London: Collier Macmillan Publishers.

Stewart, Rosemary (1967), *Managers and Their Jobs*, London: Macmillan.

Stewart, Rosemary (1991), *Managing Today and Tomorrow*, London: Macmillan.

Swartz, Stephen (1989), "The Challenges of Multi-Disciplinary Consulting to Family-Owned Businesses, *Family Business Review*, Vol. 2, No. 4, Winter.

Taylor, Frederick W. (1947), *Scientific Management*, New York: Harper & Row.

*Tichy, Noel M. and Mary Anne Devanna (1986), *The Transformational Leader*, New York: John Wiley & Sons.

Timmons, J.A., L.E. Smollen and A.L.M. Dingee (1977), *New Venture Creation*, Homewood, IL: Irwin.

Tregoe, Benjamin B. et al. (1990), "The Driving Force", *Planning Review*, March–April.

Usher, Dan (1981), *The Economic Prerequisite to Democracy*, Oxford: Basil Blackwell.

Vasconcellos e Sá, Jorge (1989), "Does Your Strategy Pass the No Test?", *European Management Journal*, Vol. 7, No. 2.

Wack, Pierre (1985), "Scenarios: Shooting the Rapids", *Harvard Business Review*, November–December.

Warner, Alan and David Arnold (1986), "Navigating the Strategic Maze", *Management Decision*, Vol. 24, No. 6.

*Washburn, Katherine and John Thornton (eds.) (1996), *Dumbing Down*, New York: W.W. Norton & Company.

*Weinshall, Theodore D. and Yael-Anna Raveh (1983), *Managing Growing Organisations: A New Approach*, Chichester: John Wiley & Sons.

Weinshall, Theodore D. and Harry C. Kyriasis (1986), "Behavioural Aspects of Outsiders Helping Managements to Improve Their Organisations", paper presented to the International Association of Applied Psychology conference, Jerusalem: July.

Wild, Ray (ed.) (1982), *How to Manage: 123 World Experts Analyse the Art of Management*, London: Heinemann.

*Wills, Gordon (1993), *Your Enterprise School of Management*, Bradford: MCB University Press Limited.

Windle, Ralph (1994), *The Poetry of Business Life*, San Francisco: Berrett-Koehler Publishers.

INDEX

Studies, the (cont'd)
  verbatim views, 60, 80, 81–
    104, 128–31, 139–43, 200,
    212–17
  see also organisations;
    Reports
style, 56, 140, 150, 152–3, 156,
  158, 161, 165, 216
  management by decree, 46
  management by slogan, 4
  management by walking
    around (MBWA), 93
  hands-on management, 91,
    93
  macho management, 45–6,
    193
  prescriptive, 53, 117, 146
succession, 153, 159, 170
Swartz, Stephen, 54
SWOT analysis, 54, 146

Taylor, Frederick W., 10
teamwork, 38, 111, 127, 213
Teare, Richard, *xi*
technology, 5, 13, 110, 163, 181,
  208, 215
Thurber, James, 242
Total Quality Management
  (TQM), 243
trade unions, 15, 19, 20, 247

training, 74–5, 154, 160, 215,
  216
trust, 46, 60, 61, 65, 72, 96, 218,
  231
truth, 10, 37, 38, 46, 61–2, 69,
  80, 95–7, 246

uncertainty, 154, 161, 163, 186,
  187, 188, 189, 190, 225, 242
unemployment, 17
unfreedom, 2, 3, 13; *see also*
  freedom
University College Dublin
  (UCD), *xi*, 47, 231
unstuckness, 41–2

values, 7, 96, 164, 237, 240
vision, 66, 76, 83–4, 102, 105–6,
  116–17, 132, 142, 165, 193,
  198, 213, 216, 225, 226, 243

Warner, Alan, 146
Weinshall, Theodore D., 62
Whitaker, T.K., 14, 15, 72
Williamson, Peter, 210
Wills, Gordon, *xi*, 246
women CEOs, 7
Wooldridge, Adrian, 77
work, 39, 234, 236, 237–9

youth, 168, 177